RESTORATION

of the

RESTORATION

The Beginnings
of the Journey

Susan Evans McCloud

CFI
An imprint of Cedar Fort, Inc.
Springville, Utah

This is not an official publication of The Church of Jesus Christ of Latter-day Saints. The opinions and views expressed herein belong solely to the author and do not necessarily represent the opinions or views of Cedar Fort, Inc. Permission for the use of sources, graphics, and photos is also solely the responsibility of the author.

ISBN 13: 978-1-4621-3819-7

Published by CFI, an imprint of Cedar Fort, Inc.
2373 W. 700 S., Springville, UT, 84663
Distributed by Cedar Fort, Inc., www.cedarfort.com

LIBRARY OF CONGRESS CONTROL NUMBER: 2020946479

Cover design by Shawnda T. Craig
Cover design © 2020 Cedar Fort, Inc.

10 9 8 7 6 5 4 3 2 1

CONTENTS

DESTINY

As the drops of rain, quiet and alone,
Fall one by one upon the thirsting earth,
And in their gathered strength become a source
Of seed and green, of sustenance and birth;

As a few faint stars pierce the black expanse—
First one to brave the night, so sure its glow—
Transcending even deepest hidden dark,
So do the shining souls embark:

I've been saved until this latter day,
Sent now, for I have a work to do,
And so I'll remember who I am
And, even though alone, against great evil stand
In joy and patience free,
Fulfilling my destiny.

—SUSAN EVANS MCCLOUD
Used with permission, LDS Intellectual Reserve

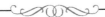

PALMYRA,
NEW YORK

Palmyra, New York, was first settled in January of 1789 by John Swift, and known in the beginning as Swift's Landing. John Swift built the first grist mill and donated land for the first church, first schoolhouse, and first burial ground. His son Asa was the first white male born in the town. Palmyra is known, above all, for its "Mormon history," but Winston Churchill's maternal grandfather, Leonard Jerome, lived and worked in Palmyra for many years. He and Clarissa Hall were married April 5, 1849, in the Palmyra Presbyterian Church. The Erie Canal was completed up to Palmyra in 1822, about the time the Smiths moved to the area. The canal crossed State Street and ran into a large basin area. At one time Palmyra was known as "the Queen of Erie Canal Towns," and it was an exciting and lively time to be living there. It was this advanced system of travel that brought great wealth to Palmyra and this area for a season. Many large and impressive homes and businesses were built, and the city progressed more than it would have without the canal.

The Smiths lived also for a time in the village of Manchester, located about eight or nine miles from Palmyra.

LUCY MACK SMITH

Part One

Lucy Mack was born in Gilsum, New Hampshire, on July 8, 1775. She was the youngest of eight children, with four older brothers and three older sisters. Lucy had a strong, clear-thinking mind and a tender heart—whose tenderness was much tried by the deaths of her two older sisters, Lovina and Lovisa, who both died of consumption. They were born a year apart, and died within months of one another.

Lovisa was married, but the care of Lovina fell largely upon Lucy, who was but fifteen years old. Fifteen through eighteen; those were the years the girl devoted to the sister she loved.

The lives and deaths of these two sisters had a profound effect upon the spiritual development of Lucy, for both women were remarkably spiritual in nature, experiencing dreams and visions in the midst of their tribulations and influencing others toward faith in Christ. They shared these remarkable experiences and the testimonies they gained freely with friends and family. And, of course, they had a particularly powerful impact upon their sensitive young sister, for Lucy actually watched Lovina die.

It is easy to see why Lucy's older brother, Stephen, urged her to pay a prolonged visit to his home in Tunbridge, Vermont. There he could pamper her a little and divert her mind from the gloom and grief of the last many months she had endured.

Lucy stayed with her brother for a year, and during that time she met and was courted by Joseph Smith, who came from an interesting and well-respected family whom her brother knew well. Lucy married Joseph in January 1796, when he was twenty-four years old and she was twenty.

George Washington was still president of the United States. The two were making a new start in a country that was doing the same thing.[1]

It was a happy marriage, blessed in the beginning with the security of a farm to work, and the extravagant wedding gift of $500 from Lucy's brother, Stephen—matched and thus doubled by his business partner, to the very impressionable sum of $1,000.

This could be the end of a lead-in to a successful and ordinary marriage, much like many others. But that was not to be the case. The Lord had plans for this young couple, and ease and affluence would not teach, refine, and prepare them as trials and adversity would.

After six happy years the couple rented their farm and moved to the nearby city of Randolph, where the first two sons, Alvin and Hyrum, were born.

But after only a few months in their new home, Lucy realized, to her horror, that a severe cold and fever she was suffering were confirmed by a doctor as the dreaded consumption.

No one can imagine the torturing thoughts and memories that passed through her mind. Her mother, quickly sent for, watched over her day and night, yet, as Lucy describes it: "I grew so weak that I could not bear the noise of a footfall except in stocking feet, nor a word to be spoken in the room except in whispers."[2] Perhaps aggravating these conditions was the fact that Lucy was already pregnant with her daughter, Sophronia.

After being agitated by the visit of a Methodist exhorter, Lucy realized with dread that she was not prepared to die: "For I do not know the ways of Christ." She strained her eyes toward a light behind the veil that seemed to cover her eyes. But shortly after this her husband came to her in tears and cried, "Oh, Lucy! My wife! You must die. The doctors have given you up, and all say you cannot live."[3]

Then alone, and in the anguish of her own soul, Lucy pled with the Lord to spare her life. Her sisters' experiences must have given her a fine measure of faith in the power and love of her Father in Heaven.

Through the long hours of the night she labored, hovering between this world and the next, thinking on her husband and children, until she approached with sure confidence the throne of grace: "I covenanted with God that if he would let me live, I would endeavor to get that religion that would enable me to serve him right, whether it was in the Bible or wherever it might be found, *even if it was to be obtained from heaven by prayer and faith.*

"At last a voice spoke to me and said, 'Seek, and ye shall find; knock, and it shall be opened unto you. Let your heart be comforted. Ye believe in god, believe also in me.'"

When her mother entered the room a few minutes later, she exclaimed in amazement at how changed Lucy looked.

"Yes, Mother," Lucy spoke, "the Lord will let me live. If I am faithful to my promise which I have made to him, he will suffer me to remain to comfort the hearts of my mother, my husband, and my children."[4]

Lucy treasured these things in her heart, and many times pondered them through the remarkably wondrous and uncommon experiences of her coming life.

But Lucy was also a woman of action, and she wasted no time. She wrote that "the subject of religion occupied my mind continually."[5] But she was not to find answers, satisfaction, nor peace for a very long time, despite her tireless efforts. At length, after attending meetings of various religions, listening and hungering, going away "grieved and troubled," she determined that "there is not on earth the religion which I seek. I must turn to my Bible, take Jesus and his disciples for an example, and try to obtain from God that which man cannot give nor take away."[6]

Lucy was as assuredly worthy and prepared for her role as the mother of the Prophet Joseph, as Mary was for her sacred calling as the mother of the Savior.

Perhaps without truly realizing it, Lucy had now placed the course of her future life into hands higher than her own. And very shortly she saw the work of the Almighty, difficult as it was to understand or accept.

A very popular and profitable enterprise at this time was the crystallizing and exporting of the ginseng root, which had an immense value in China particularly, where it was apparently a great remedy for the plague. Joseph made the six-day journey to New York City and arranged for his ginseng to be taken to China aboard a ship just getting ready to set sail. Under written obligation, the captain promised to sell the crop and return the profits to him.

However, a Mr. Stevens, a merchant in their vicinity, had urged Joseph to sell his crop to him for a price so much below its value that he refused. Angered, Stevens hurried to New York, identified the vessel, and secured a berth for his son who, upon arrival in China, sold Joseph's ginseng at great profit as his own!

The bitter disappointment and the desolation of this loss caused nearly utter ruin for the young couple. Joseph Smith still had debts he had hoped to clear with his profit, which had now ceased to exist. They were living on the farm in Tunbridge at this time, which they sold for half its value in order to pay their Boston debts. All this time Lucy had held onto the thousand-dollar wedding gift, which she now drew forth and presented to her husband. To part with the farm she loved, and to part with the security of her cared-for money, must have smote her heart.

Her brother Colonel Mack kindly took their gathered funds to Boston, discharged the debts, and returned with the receipts which, as Lucy put it, "set us free from the embarrassment of debt, but not from the embarrassment of poverty."[7]

Lucy's further response to this hardship shows us the tenor of both her mind and her heart: "Although we might be poor, we would have the satisfaction of knowing that we had given no man any cause of complaint, and having a conscience void of offense, the society of our children, and the blessing of health, we still might be happy indeed."[8]

This sentiment, so deeply felt, sustained Lucy through the years of brutal, devastating trials which she and her beloved family endured.

Part Two

Only a complete biography of Lucy Mack Smith could begin to do justice to her life's experiences, especially as they are parallel, and so intertwined, with those of her Prophet son.

After leaving the Tunbridge area, Lucy and her family moved to Royalton, Vermont, where a son, Ephraim, was born, and died as an infant. William was also born in Royalton, being the third living son—all of whom were born on March 13.

Things were going well. Joseph Sr. had even received the first of a series of dreams which would open up his spiritual sensations—the very thing Lucy had been praying for.

But a typhoid epidemic swept through the area, killing a devastating six thousand people, most of them children.

Lucy's little Sophronia struggled for just shy of three months. Then the doctor shook his head and gave her up for lost. Lucy did not accept the death of her daughter. She and Joseph knelt at her bedside and prayed.

Knowing that the Lord had heard her plea, Lucy lifted her daughter up and walked the floor with her, until she began to breathe freely in her arms!

But her near-death was only a prelude to what little seven-year-old Joseph suffered, as his infection shot suddenly into his shoulder with excruciating pain. Then, after the doctor lanced a fever sore, the pain went down his side and into the marrow of the bone of his leg.

The boy's sufferings, as well as Joseph and Lucy's, were so severe that only through the aid of heaven could they get through. Gentle Hyrum sat day and night by his brother's bed, holding the most painful parts of Joseph's leg, with the patience and love that was to characterize him throughout his life. Lucy records that this dedicated help "enabled the little sufferer the better to bear the pain which otherwise *seemed almost ready to take his life.*"[9]

Lucy fought like a fierce mother lion for the well-being of her son. Through her insistence, Joseph's leg was not removed, but a rare operation performed, and Joseph survived—but was so thin and weakened that Lucy could carry him easily as she went about the house.

Exhausted in body and means, Lucy and Joseph suffered the devastating crop failures that struck Vermont. At last they made plans to move to upstate New York—placing themselves where the Lord intended them to be.

In every phase of Lucy's life she was what you might describe as determined, fearless, and filled with faith.

The driver who had been hired to take them to Vermont turned surly, even cruel—especially toward young Joseph who still limped painfully—and then he brazenly attempted to throw out all of the family's things and steal Lucy's cart.

She roundly condemned him before the audience in the inn, took her children, and continued the long journey on her own, with no help at all. Although she had but a few cents in her pocket, she arrived safely in Palmyra, overjoyed to be with her husband again.

And then? Then Lucy went forth with her usual cheerfulness and zest for life. She made friends with her neighbors. She painted oilcloth coverings for floors and tables, thus making a little of the money they so badly needed. The local women came quickly to admire her, and be impressed by the helpful, kindly manners of her family.

In Palmyra Lucy at last united herself with the Presbyterian Church; interestingly, this took place in February of 1820—after sixteen years of seeking for the truth.

Throughout these years Lucy taught her children by example to take their questions, perplexities, and troubles to the Lord in prayer. She taught them obedience and reverence to God, as her mother had taught her. In fact, she often sought out a spot—usually in a wooded, solitary area some distance from the house—where the members of her family could go alone to commune with God.

Thus it was natural—in this same early spring of 1820—for Joseph to go to the woods which were at some little distance from his father's house, and kneel in prayer.

We have not space in this current work to treat with any degree of thoroughness the Vision in the Grove, or the range of phenomenal changes that at once began in the lives of Joseph and his entire family. We do know that Lucy, his mother, is the first person he approached and spoke to after he returned from the Grove.

Knowing her son well, she ascertained that something of some importance had happened, and she questioned him. He was unable to explain; he was scarcely able to speak. But his response is interesting, for he said: "Never mind; all is well—I am well enough off." Then he added: "I have learned for myself that Presbyterianism is not true" (Joseph Smith—History 1:5–20).

As experiences continued, as Moroni appeared and introduced himself to Joseph, Lucy and the entire family united in harmonious love and support of what was happening, of all that was being brought forth, strange and marvelous as it may be.

Constant danger surrounded Joseph, and cruel, almost inhuman, things were suffered by his family as well. But Lucy and Joseph Sr. never complained nor faltered.

And there were happy family times as well. The family would hurry through their daily work so that they might gather round Joseph and hear what he had to tell them, for he was given knowledge and instruction often, from day to day. He would teach them from what he, himself, had been given—and more. In Lucy's words, "In the course of our evening conversations, Joseph gave us some of the most amusing recitals which could be imagined. He would describe the ancient inhabitants of this continent, their dress, their manner of traveling, the animals which they rode, the cities that they built . . . their mode of warfare, and their religious worship as specifically as though he had spent his life among them."[10]

Unique indeed was the life the Lord had prepared for them, and which, with heart and mind, they were willing to accept.

About this same time, Alvin had reached the age of twenty-five and was engaged to be married. But mid-morning on November 15, 1823, Alvin was suddenly overcome by a pain so severe that he quit his work, made his way to the house, and asked his father to send for the doctor.

Sadly, their own trusted physician was not in town, and the one from the neighboring village was unknown to them. He gave the suffering boy a heavy dose of calomel—even though Alvin objected to it! The medication lodged in his stomach, and no efforts could dislodge it. "You cannot move it," Alvin said. "Consequently, it must take my life."[11]

Knowing his time was very brief, Alvin called for his family and gave each person a loving blessing and farewell. To Joseph he said: "I am going to die now. I want you to be a good boy and do everything that lies in your power to obtain the record. Be faithful in receiving instruction and in keeping every commandment that is given you. Your brother Alvin must now leave you, but remember the example which he has set for you, and set a good example for the children . . . always be kind to Father and Mother."[12]

The excruciating grief this family suffered cannot be described. Alvin was a Christ-like young man; everyone loved him, everyone trusted and depended upon him. He was Lucy's strength in many ways, and her hope for the future. Bitter, bitter was the sorrow of the little family—and of the community as well. Their seventy-year-old doctor was outraged by the unnecessary tragedy. He told the people: "Here is one of the loveliest youth that ever trod the streets of Palmyra destroyed, murdered as it were, by him at whose hand relief was expected, cast off from the face of the earth by a careless quack who even dared to trifle with the life of a fellow mortal."[13]

This deep sorrow was to accompany Lucy for the rest of her life, and Alvin's pure spirit often blessed his brothers in their challenges and struggles.

After avoiding a cruel deception to take Joseph Sr. and Lucy's home away from them, Lucy prepared for the marriage of Hyrum to Jerusha Barden on November 2, 1826. Joseph and Emma were married in January 1827—and now Lucy's two oldest surviving sons had taken that step into adulthood which would remove them, in a subtle, but very real way, from her and her care.

The years of waiting and of preparation for Joseph were over. On September 20, 1827, Emma accompanied her new husband to the Hill Cumorah. It was night. Lucy had things to keep her hands busy, and she could not sleep. She spent the hours while Joseph was gone in prayer, and the following morning was very tense until she learned that Joseph was all right, and that his errand to the still, dark hill had been a success.

There ensued a period of new challenges and wonders for all the Smith family: trying to keep the plates safe, as well as Joseph; trying to get the freedom in which a translation could take place; trying to find means whereby the Book of Mormon could be printed—when the organization of the Church could be actually and legally made—and throughout all this and more, Lucy was an active participant. Indeed, Lucy spent one long night alone with the manuscript, which was hidden beneath the headboard of her bed. Many different impressions, memories, and spiritual experiences came to her during those hours, so that she exclaimed, "Thus I spent the night surrounded by enemies and yet in any ecstasy of happiness. Truly I can say that my soul did magnify and my spirit rejoiced in God, my Savior."[14]

Some stories from Lucy's life would be important to include here. One is the very real miracle that Lucy's faith brought to pass.

Literally hundreds of people were joining the Church in the Kirtland, Ohio, area, and Joseph was being urged to move the main body of the Saints there.

Lucy found herself in charge of taking the large group of the Waterloo Branch to Kirtland—some eighty souls, which included babies and children.

Once aboard the canal boat, Lucy realized that many of the people had come ill-prepared; so she shared her own provisions with them. She organized hymn singing and prayers twice daily. She scolded and attempted to organize the women who were being slothful in keeping watch over their children.

"We cannot get our children to mind," they complained.

"I could make them mind me easily enough," Lucy countered. "And since you will not control them, I shall."

She organized the children with songs and games as well as a form of lessons, and they all responded to her authority and her love.

Several crises came and were endured, culminating in the boat being locked in ice, and unable to move.

"Where is your confidence in God?" she admonished the men and their wives. "Do you not know that all things are in His hands, that He made all things and overrules them? If every Saint here would just lift their desires to Him in prayer, that the way might be opened before us, how easy it would be for God to cause the ice to break away, and in a moment's time we could be off on our journey."[15]

It happened according to her words, and she became almost a legend and a wonder to the early Saints.

The years in Kirtland were brief, but they were filled with many blessings. Prime among these was the purchase of the Egyptian mummies and papyrus, brought by a Mr. Chandler, and their subsequent translation by Joseph.

There were always challenges: "droves of company," as Lucy put it, nonmembers as well as members of the Church.[16]

There was the treacherous and dangerous journey of Zion's Camp to Missouri, in hopes of assisting and redeeming the imperiled Saints there. When cholera struck the camp, their journey was slowed and delayed. Lucy, her husband, and others became concerned.

The two brothers, Joseph and Hyrum, in the midst of their sufferings, took turns praying, entreating the Lord to relieve them. As they knelt, Hyrum suddenly sprang to his feet. "Joseph, we shall return," he cried, "for I have seen an open vision in which I saw Mother on her knees under an apple tree praying for us, and she is even now asking God, in tears, to spare our lives. The Spirit testifies to me that her prayers and ours shall be heard."[17]

"Oh my mother," Joseph said later, "how often have your prayers been a means of assisting us when the shadows of death encompassed us."[18]

The crowning achievement of the Kirtland days was the building of the temple—the first temple on the earth in this last dispensation of time. Great were the spiritual wonders: angels singing, appearing on the roof of the building, small children testifying, the Apostle Peter attending the dedication, and many actually seeing the Savior in vision.

But following this a spirit of speculation and a great apostasy took place. The Prophet's life was in danger, and so was Brigham Young's for standing firmly beside him. More than sixteen hundred Saints fled the city, and Joseph Sr. and Lucy Mack Smith were among them.

One of the most powerful, insightful stories of Lucy concerns the family's sad journey from Kirtland to Missouri, which was a daunting distance of close to one thousand miles.

They left with two of their sons in May of 1838, driving through rain and storm, one night lying all night in the rain, another seeking shelter in a wretched little hut. Lucy became very ill—the quilted skirt which she wore for three days wringing wet. Soon after crossing the Mississippi River her daughter, Catherine, gave birth to a son.

Leaving mother, baby, and husband with daughter Sophronia for help, the rest traveled on. Lucy, coughing continually, was no longer able to ride in a sitting position, nor travel more than four miles a day.

A firm impression came to her that if she could find a secluded place where she might call upon the Lord, she would be healed. She urged her husband to press on for Huntsville and, when they stopped here, Lucy tells us in her own words:

> By the aid of staffs I reached a fence, and then followed the fence some distance till I came to a dense hazel thicket. Here I threw myself on the ground and thought it was no matter how far I was from the house, for if the Lord would not hear me and I must die, I might as well die here as anywhere.
>
> When I was a little rested, I commenced calling upon the Lord to beseech his mercy, praying for my health and the life of my daughter, Catherine. I urged every claim which the scriptures give us, and was as humble as I knew how to be, and *I continued praying near three hours.*
>
> At last I was entirely relieved from pain, my cough left me, and I was well. Moreover, I received an assurance that I should hear from my daughter about the middle of the same day. I arose and went to the house *in as good health as I ever enjoyed.*
>
> The day after (Catherine) came, I washed a very large quality of clothes with as much ease as though I had not been out of health at all.[19]

The power was within Lucy herself; the power, of faith, testimony, and prayer. The Lord, as she felt and knew, had bestowed it upon her.

Part Three

The spirit of the adversary, engendering cruelty and persecution, did not take long to raise its head. After a few months of peace, an election was held at Gallatin, the county seat. The Saints were attacked and harassed, and when some attempted to defend themselves, the word went out that Joseph Smith had killed seven men at that place!

Lucy, calmly going about her business in Far West, heard of this only when a large body of soldiers entered the city and the officers approached her house, demanding that she give up the Prophet.

Lucy was calm, polite, and possessed with the assurance which the Spirit gave her. She invited the men in and said if they were there to kill the Mormons as they were boasting, then they may as well begin with her.

Joseph, who had been writing letters in the next room, entered, and she introduced the men to him. In his pleasant, easy manner he sat and talked with them, telling of all the Mormons had suffered, then calmly told Lucy that Emma would be expecting him, and he would go on home.

In Lucy's words:

> At this, two of the men sprang to their feet saying, "You shall not go alone, for it is not safe. We will go with you and guard you." Joseph thanked them and they left with him.
>
> While they were absent, the remainder of the officers stood by the door, and I overheard the following conversation between them: FIRST OFFICER: "Did you not feel something strange when Smith took you by the hand? I never felt so in my life."
> SECOND OFFICER: "I felt as though I could not move. I would not harm one hair of that man's head for the whole world."[20]

The conversation continued but, for our purposes, this is sufficient. Joseph was of the same ilk, the same spiritual substance as his mother and oh, how she must have loved him!

Conditions in Missouri worsened, until there was a frenzy of madness, with the mobbers even setting fire to their own huts in order to claim cruelty from the Mormons. On October 26, 1838, Governor Boggs issued the infamous order: "The Mormons must be treated as enemies and must be exterminated or driven from the state."[21] Twelve hundred had already been burned out and driven from Jackson County. Now, with the authority of the governor, the Haun's Mill Massacre took place, with atrocities beyond belief.

Meanwhile, an army of two thousand men was surrounding Far West, outnumbering the citizens in the city four to one!

On October 31, Joseph and several of his brethren were betrayed to the mob. Then a true nightmare for Joseph Sr. and Lucy began.

The city was drenched by rain, and then besieged by enemies, and the imprisoned men, in the midst of their enemies, were constantly under threat of their lives. The mobsters were like wild beasts, hungry for the blood of the Prophet. As Lucy described it:

"No tongue can ever express the sound that was conveyed to our ears, nor the sensations that were produced in our hearts. It was like the screeching of a hundred owls mingled with the howling of an army of bloodhounds and the screaming of a thousand panthers all famishing for the prey which had been torn piecemeal among them."

Joseph Sr. could not endure it, and fell nearly senseless on the bed.[22]

How did Lucy endure it? Very possibly the night she had been told she was to die—the night she had made a solemn covenant with the Lord that she would comfort the hearts of her husband and children—perhaps this came back vividly to sustain her; it seems very possible that this might have been so.

Indeed, when Joseph and Hyrum were roughly shoved into a wagon to be taken only heaven knew where, Lucy grabbed her daughter Lucy and fought her way through a mass of soldiers "brandishing pistols, swords, and all sorts of weapons and threatening in foul language to knock us down and drive over us where we stood."[23]

"I am the mother of the Prophet," she cried and made her way to the wagon at last. She saw Joseph and was able to reach out and touch his hand. With a sob he cried, "God bless you, Mother!"[24]

She also received, "by the gift of prophecy: 'Let your heart be comforted concerning your children, for they shall not harm a hair of their heads' . . . This relieved my mind, and I was prepared to comfort my children."[25]

Lucy and her family were to find peace and the refuge of a home in Nauvoo. But there were still many struggles and heart-rending trials to get through.

The cumbersome, painful journey following the cruel destruction and forced desertion of their home in Far West was as wrenching as the journey from Kirtland had been. There were many difficulties, including their horses being wind-broken, meaning that they had to trudge up hills themselves; days of travel in cold rain; people along their forlorn path who refused them shelter, so that they often slept on the ground, without even a fire for comfort and warmth.

Six miles from the Mississippi the mud was deep and sticky. When they reached the river, the snow that had been falling was now six inches deep. There was no hope of shelter, so they made their beds on the snow, lay down, and attempted to get some rest.[26]

Listed here are only a few of the struggles, which continued on into Quincy, Illinois, and through the early days of Nauvoo, when Lucy suffered from very poor health and the ravages of "a severe case of cholera—so severe that it 'seemed to be almost bursting the bones themselves asunder.'"[27]

Nauvoo provided peace, blessings, and quiet joys for Lucy, but there were still many struggles and heart-rending trials to go through, and she was, as always, required to watch as Joseph never obtained more than snatches of peace, nor freedom from the malignity of those who hated and persecuted him.

But on September 14, 1840, at the age of sixty-nine, Joseph Smith Sr. died. He was Patriarch to the Church, and the people loved him. The devastation of sorrow for Lucy seemed to break her heart. They had always wanted to, somehow, die together. But in Joseph Sr.'s last words he told her, "You must stay to comfort the children when I am gone."[28]

That word again; the word of promise. What must Lucy have thought?

Lucy, having injured her knee, was sick and low all winter. Then, at the end of January of the new year 1841, Samuel's wife, Mary Ann, died suddenly. Don Carlos died on August 7, and on the first day of September Robert B. Thompson, Hyrum's brother-in-law and husband to Mercy Fielding, died of the same disease, called quick consumption.

Death and loss continued. Two weeks later Joseph's youngest son, named after Don Carlos, died after suffering terribly. Two brief weeks passed, and Hyrum's second son, also named Hyrum, died of a fever.[29]

Life must somehow go on. But we wonder how the Smith family made it through that year. Each succeeding year was stippled with persecutions and even more family deaths. In October 1843, "Sophronia, second daughter of Don Carlos, died of the scarlet fever, leaving her widowed mother doubly desolate."[30]

Through it all, Lucy suffered seasons of desolating sickness that threatened to take her life. It was the strength of her spirit which had power to subdue the flesh.

In her history, Lucy gives in detail the events surrounding the deaths of Joseph and Hyrum. She records the reactions of the widows and children when her sons' bodies were laid out in death. Of herself at this time she said:

> I had for a long time braced every nerve, roused every energy of my soul, and called upon God to strengthen me, but when I entered the

room and saw my murdered sons extended both at once before my eyes and heard the sobs and groans of my family . . . it was too much. I sank back, crying to God in the agony of my soul, "My God, my God, why hast thou forsaken this family?"

Where Joseph and Hyrum had gone, they would be with their beloved father and brother, Alvin. But Lucy was alone, to face this unbelievable horror and loss.

But a voice replied to her anguished cries, saying, "I have taken them to myself, that they might have rest."[31]

* * *

Lucy supported the reorganization of the Church under Brigham Young from the very start. She knew the mantle of her son had fallen upon Brigham and the Twelve. She received her ordinances of endowment in December of 1845. The Nauvoo City Charter was illegally revoked, and the people, especially in outlying areas, were contending with persecutions again. The spirit of gathering was upon the people; Lucy must have felt it. All of Nauvoo was turned into wagon and wheelwright shops as the Saints prepared to leave for a place unknown.

But Samuel, too, had died, after great suffering, at the end of July. She had raised six sons. Now only one remained, and he was estranged, and would, in time, be excommunicated from the Church.

What this one noble woman carried with her in her mind and her heart, we cannot presume to realize.

"I feel the Lord will let Brother Brigham take the people away," Lucy said.[32] And, letting her feelings overtake her, she expressed her desire to go with the body of the Saints. The people were overjoyed to think of having Mother Smith with them. But, bit by bit, Lucy faced the realities. Emma would not go; she was in no state, physically or mentally, to do so. Lucy's daughters, too, were here, in Nauvoo, married and settled.

Lucy's choices became nothing but insubstantial shadows now. Had she not promised the Lord that she would care for and comfort her family? She was in the City of Joseph, where her dead were buried. This must be where she belonged.

For a while she lived with her daughter, Lucy, seventy miles from Nauvoo. But she returned to live out her days with Emma in the Prophet's Mansion House.

The past was with her every breath that she drew, and people were still drawn to her. Visitors found themselves asking her questions, and listening. "She pronounced a blessing upon many of them as they passed on their way; a blessing in her own words, brought forth from the fonts of heaven; a mother's blessing."[33]

Lucy died May 14, 1856. She was eighty-one years old. She stood at the ushering in of the dispensation of the fulness of times, beside her husband and her sons. Her nobility, her courage, and her faithfulness have become the hallmark of all loving and worthy Latter-day Saints. Lucy was Mother of a People, as well as mother of the Prophet of God.

ENDNOTES

1. Smith, *History of Joseph Smith*, 440.
2. Ibid., 47.
3. Ibid., 48.
4. Ibid.
5. Ibid.
6. Ibid., 50.
7. Ibid., 53.
8. Ibid.
9. Ibid., 73, emphasis added.
10. Ibid., 112.
11. McCloud, *Stories of Lucy Mack Smith*, 33.
12. Ibid., 34.
13. Ibid.
14. Ibid., 40.
15. Smith, 268.
16. McCloud, *Stories of Lucy Mack Smith*, 52.
17. Ibid., 51–52.
18. Smith, 319.
19. Ibid., 358–359.
20. Ibid., 363.
21. McCloud, *Joseph Smith, A Photobiography*, 85.
22. Ibid., 87.
23. Smith, 406.
24. Ibid., 407.
25. McCloud, *Stories of Lucy Mack Smith*, 64.
26. Ibid., 66–67.
27. Smith 419.
28. Ibid., 436.
29. Ibid., 444, 445.
30. Ibid., Smith, 449.
31. Ibid., Smith, 457.
32. McCloud, *An Inspiring Personal Biography*, 127.
33. McCloud, *Stories of Lucy Mack Smith*, 85.

EMMA HALE SMITH

JOSEPH WAS DRAWN TO THIS girl from the very first. Working for her father, he had opportunities to watch her. He was drawn to her stately beauty, the way she carried herself, the richness of her singing voice, and the vitality of her mind. As his mother, Lucy, expressed: "Joseph thought that no young woman that he ever was acquainted with was better calculated to render the man of her choice happy than Miss Emma Hale."[1]

Emma was twenty-one years old to Joseph's nineteen. When she decided to say yes to his insistent importuning, which continued for the space of two years, she knew what she would be facing at home. Joseph was a nobody as far as her father was concerned; an uneducated day laborer with few prospects. He was young, and he had strange notions and ideas. Isaac Hale was respected and wealthy, one of the wealthiest men in the Susquehanna Valley.[2] He wanted his beautiful daughter to marry someone on par with himself.

Born on July 10, 1804, Emma was the seventh child of a family of nine. She enjoyed many privileges and improved upon them. She loved to ride horses, swim, and play with her brothers. Yet she possessed many homemaking skills and was an excellent cook. Emma was also the most educated of her siblings, doing an extra year of schooling beyond grammar school.[3]

Her father knew all this, and he knew of her fine mind and deep spiritual sensibilities. In 1812, when Emma was, interestingly, eight years old, a Methodist circuit rider had come through Harmony preaching and encouraging the children to go into the woods alone and pray to the Lord. Emma acted on his advice and was kneeling in the woods praying when her father came upon her and listened to the fervent force of her prayer, to "the wailings of her young heart in his behalf."⁴ Her child's faith helped him to seek faith in the Savior, which he had not done before.

Joseph, during the two years of working and waiting, attended several schools and improved his education. "A neighbor said of him that 'his character was irreproachable; that he was well known for truth and uprightness; that he moved in the first circles of the community, and he was often spoken of as a young man of intelligence, and good morals, and possessing a mind susceptible of the highest intellectual attainments.'"⁵

Surely Emma also noticed these qualities in Joseph. And, surely, he spoke to her of himself and what he had experienced at the hands of the Lord; of the Sacred Grove, of Moroni, of the many spiritual manifestations he had enjoyed, and perhaps of the extent of the kingdom which the Lord would require him to build.

She must have learned, too, of the trials and atrocities he had suffered, and perhaps been gently told that such would be his lot throughout his life.

But she chose, and went with him to the home of Squire Tarbill in South Bainbridge, where they were married secretly on January 18, 1827. Thus, in the stroke of a brush, she gave up her own life, sacrificed all that was dear to her, and united her fate with his.

At first they went to live with Joseph's parents in Manchester, New York, so they would be in place for the culmination of Joseph's four years of learning and obedience. On September 21, 1827, she accompanied her young husband to the Hill Cumorah, where the gold plates were at last given into his safekeeping. Interrupting the drive home, Joseph stopped and hid the plates in a hollow tree. Emma carried the plates and interpreters, covered only by a silk handkerchief, on her lap.

The ensuing days and weeks were filled with the most intense fears and anxieties. In early December, near the end of the year, they moved back to Harmony, where they worked to support themselves, living at first in a small attached kitchen of her parents' home, later moving to a frame home which they purchased from Emma's brother Jesse, just across the road from her parents' house.

Surely the hearts of her family were somehow softened by the Lord during this crucial time when their help was so critically needed by the young couple.

Joseph began to translate the Book of Mormon, and Emma acted as his scribe. Martin Harris came to them and was given characters from the

Book of Mormon to take to specialists in New York. From the beginning his involvement engendered conflict and difficulties—and his wife, nearly demented, was against her husband's support of the Prophet, and determined to see and get her hands on the plates for herself. Martin's wife horrified Emma by ransacking her home in search of them, and spreading falsehoods and alarms throughout the neighborhood.

Martin promised to go home to Palmyra, but somehow entreated Joseph into letting him take the 116 page manuscript which had been translated with him—to prove to his crazed wife the validity of the work. He left on June 14, 1828.

The following day Emma's baby was born—a tiny boy, whom they immediately named Alvin. But he did not survive his birth, and Emma became so ill that she "hovered between life and death."[6]

The anguish of their loss and Joseph's deep concern for his wife were compounded bitterly by Martin's loss of the 116 pages! The plates were taken from Joseph for a spell, and he spent his somewhat dreary, repentant time in working the farm he had bought from Emma's father. But this was a good healing and fallow time for them both.

In April 1829 Oliver Cowdery entered their lives. The work began again in earnest. "Oliver wrote 'almost without cessation' for several weeks."[7] But, how do you live without food, the very basics of life? Joseph Knight came to their rescue, bringing grain, tea, potatoes, "'a barrel of Mackrel, and some lined paper for writing.'"[8]

Emma had been raised with ease, wealth, and countless opportunities to do what she desired, from reading to horseback riding. The shock of this kind of an existence must have been great. In early June they could no longer make it, and Peter Whitmer's son, David, brought a wagon and transported them all to live and work for a spell in his father's house.

These were the beginnings of Emma's life. She had to tear herself away from her family again, and this was most hard. She had no home of her own and no idea of when she might have one, nor what her future might hold.

But the Church was actually organized in April of 1830, and Emma and the Knight family were baptized near the end of June. Even then, as always, a mob of fifty men harassed the people with rude disruptions and threats of real harm.

Joseph was to confirm Emma and the others that evening, but as the Prophet recorded: "'To my surprise, I was visited by a constable, and arrested by him on a warrant, on the charge of being a disorderly person, of setting the country in an uproar by preaching the Book of Mormon.'"[9]

The case was eventually dismissed, but Emma's confirmation did not go forward until sometime later.

It was in these most tumultuous, uncertain times that the Lord sent a special revelation to Emma—the only revelation in the scriptures addressed to a woman alone and, through her, to all of her sex.

It is a beautiful and powerful scripture which was a comfort and guidance to Emma throughout her life. The Lord told her not to fear, and to "lay aside the things of this world, and seek for the things of a better" (D&C 25:10).

She had been learning how to do this. She had been deeply tried. And she would be tried in the fire again and again.

By the end of January 1831 Joseph and Emma, and several hundred members of the Church, traveled through the snowy wilderness to Kirtland, Ohio. Three brief months later, on April 30, Emma gave birth to twins, Thaddeus and Louisa, who lived only three hours. Julia Murdock had also given birth to twins and died, leaving them motherless. So Joseph and Emma adopted these twins, naming them Joseph and Julia.

Less than a year later, however, when the babies were growing, a mob broke into their home, and little Joseph, who was already very ill, died after the intrusion of the men, who dragged the Prophet from his bed, beat him, tarred and feathered him, and left the sick baby exposed to the cold air of the March night.

Joseph exhibited to Emma a form of courage that required all the senses and all the qualities of soul she possessed. Despite being hurt and bruised, Joseph endured the cruel process of scraping the tar from his skin, and all that went with it, so that he could attend his church meeting the next morning and preach. That some members of the mob had the cruel audacity to attend that meeting must have tried Emma sorely!

In Kirtland was the School of the Prophets, and the building of the first temple since ancient times, the dedication of that temple with remarkable spiritual manifestations, visions, and blessings. But there was also Joseph and Hyrum spearheading in May of 1834 the dangerous journey of Zion's Camp, a thousand miles into Missouri, where cruel mobs awaited them.

It took much work and sacrifice to erect a temple. And Emma again was pregnant, with her baby born June 20, less than four months after the March 7 dedication. Frederick Granger Williams Smith lived, and there were a few months of peace and rejoicing for Emma and the Saints.

But speculation became rampant, and the Saints forgot the Pentecostal blessings, looking for the wealth and advantages of the world. When the National Bank Panic of 1837 hit and the Kirtland Safety Society Bank failed, it was easy to place the blame upon the Prophet. In January of 1838 Joseph was forced to leave Kirtland—alone—Emma and his family joining him in Far West, Missouri, in mid-March.

Emma was often left to face tremendous hardships and difficulties alone. There was loneliness and uncertainty—fear for Joseph—and the constant need to *ask others* for help and assistance.

February through May of 1838 were such months, and Emma, with three small children, was expecting again. But she was with Joseph and, though the going was slow, they were together, and often traveling with Brigham Young and others, who pooled their wisdom and experience in deciding how to cross the frozen Mississippi River.

It took three long, agonizing months to make the journey. Once in Missouri they faced the Salt River and the same kinds of challenges.

Emma's new home was a simple log cabin, furnished largely through the kind contributions and help of her neighbors. The Church was in turmoil, with many men who had been faithful in the beginning now being excommunicated for one reason or another.

On June 2 a son was born whom they named Alexander Hale Smith. One short factual sentence—but pregnancies, births, heart-rending infant deaths took their toll on the women of these times!

And Emma found Missouri to be no haven for the newly arrived Saints. But despite upsets, some actual conflict, and many lying accounts, there was a season of basic peace, during which Joseph was at home, working on a history of the Church, and Emma was able to take care of her children and her new baby.

However, some of the lies against the Prophet, especially those of disenchanted members, led to the cruelty for which their enemies had been itching. On October 27, 1838, Governor Boggs issued an actual Extermination Order in which he said: "The Mormons must be treated as enemies and must be exterminated or driven from the state, if necessary, for the public good."[10]

Then Emma's whole world exploded into madness. Far West became under siege of the mob. Joseph and his gentle brother, Hyrum, were handed over into the hands of murderers,

Emma's home was ransacked along with the others. Everything of value or use was taken. One of the apostates who had previously sat at her table and shared sacred moments was William McLellin. Emma asked him, "William, why are you doing this?" His reply was, "Because I can."[11]

Emma received tender communications from Joseph. "Farewell, oh, my kind and Affectionate Emma. I am yours forever. Your husband and true friend."[12]

On at least three occasions, Emma contrived to visit Joseph. And how did she contend with the horrifying, inhuman circumstances in which he was imprisoned? She proved herself noble indeed; and noble again when she left the state of Missouri.

Brigham Young organized the brethren into a solemn covenant "to stand by and assist each other to the utmost of our abilities in removing from this state, and that we will never desert the poor who are worthy, till they shall be out of the reach of the extermination order."[13] The citizens of Illinois were outraged at what had happened in Missouri and were willing to welcome the homeless wayfarers and assist them. Emma left Far West on February 7, 1838. Stephen Markham drove the wagon which carried Emma and her children, as well as the Jonathan Holmes family.

Once again Emma had to face a crossing of the frozen Mississippi. She walked across the great expanse, carrying her nine-month-old baby, her children clinging to her, and her body weighed down by Joseph's papers, and his manuscript of the Bible, hidden in her pocket apron.

Once she was safe in Quincy, Emma was given succor by the family of a Judge Cleveland and his wife, Sarah. Their home stood a little outside the town, and other families were staying with this kind family as well.[14]

Emma does not leave written record, and we wonder how such a gathering of people, crowded into the home of strangers, were able to get along and make things work, as days and weeks stretched on. The horror of the sufferings they had just passed through and the anguish of being bereft of all their earthly goods lay upon the hearts of them all. But Emma bore a deeper anguish: what would happen to her husband, and how long would he be required to endure the inhuman treatment to which he was being submitted?

On April 22, 1839, "a ragged, dirty, emaciated Joseph approached the gate of the Cleveland's house. After five long months in prison he and the others had been allowed to escape and were making their painful way back to their families. What made Emma look outside just at that moment . . . she rushed out into Joseph's arms before he could get half way up the path to the house."[15]

Commerce—renamed Nauvoo by Joseph—was the first real home Emma Smith was to have; and the last, in those days which as yet were hidden from her view.

Her first log house had only one room below and one above, and had been used as the first Indian agency in Illinois. The very early days were a blurring of sickness and fatigue, as large numbers of the Saints became ill with malaria, which infested the swampy land. Joseph, himself, was ill, yet he and Emma gave up their home and lived in a tent in their yard, where other Saints were doing the same, as well as the ones being cared for in their home! Emma had a natural skill of nursing and a gift for healing, and she gave all her care and energy to those in need.

It was here that Joseph arose from his sickbed and, taking several of the brethren with him, administered to the sick along both sides of the Mississippi.

Miracles were a part of Joseph's life and, therefore, a part of Emma's; a very, very unique way of life. Did she realize the extent of Joseph's calling? It seems that she did, for she "let go of him" far more often than she was able to hold him. Not only was the Prophet constantly in demand for matters of business in the Church, but there was also the constant organization and sending forth of missionaries, the re-institution of the printing press, the incorporation of Nauvoo and the city charter, which included the establishment of courts, and of a city military unit that was known as the Nauvoo Legion. There was the establishing and running of the new city, digging the foundation of a new temple, the welcoming—and finding place for—the literally thousands of converts arriving daily—five thousand of these, during the first six years coming from Britain alone.

Fields needed to be plowed and planted, houses and barns to be built. Nauvoo became a beehive of activity! But oh, how the hearts of the Saints must have rejoiced.

In September 1840, the patriarch, Joseph Smith Sr., died. His loss was felt deeply by all of the Saints. Lucy had a difficult time letting go of him. They had passed through trials together that had melded them into a oneness that was rare and powerful indeed.

Three months before this loss, Emma had given birth to a son named Don Carlos, after Joseph's younger brother, whom everyone loved. Her hands were full; there was always plenty for her to do. But Nauvoo was "the City Beautiful," and there were many warm, happy times as the days and months advanced. But the hatred and envy of their enemies was smoldering and waiting to again advance.

The year 1841 became a year of intense suffering and loss, beginning with the death of Samuel's wife, Mary, who died as a result of the exposures she had suffered in Missouri. In June Joseph was suddenly arrested on an order from the governor of Missouri. Although it was proven both illegal and untrue and Joseph was freed, yet the feel of persecution, like an iron band, must have closed round Emma's heart.

Then, in August Don Carlos died suddenly of quick consumption. And just over a week later little Don Carlos, Emma's beloved fourteen-month-old baby, also died.

It did not end. A month later Robert Thompson, Don Carlos' friend and co-worker, succumbed to the same disease. Robert was Hyrum's brother-in-law, being married to Mary Fielding's sister, Mercy.

There was no time to recover, scarcely time to mourn. It became horror following horror. But how did Emma survive? She hadn't expected to have this lovely and robust child taken from her. The loss of even one child can devastate a woman for a lifetime, and Emma's losses were bitter and many.

She was also living in fear so much of the time; fear and a far-reaching uncertainty, over which she had no control.

Baby Don Carlos died on August 15, 1841. So Emma must have been beginning another pregnancy, which culminated on February 6, 1842, with the birth of a son who did not survive his birth!

I suppose mortals endure what they must endure. Interestingly, a month and a half later a marvelous event took place, which expanded Emma's view of herself, of women, and of the gospel which had been restored.

In the summer of 1842 some of the sisters, Sarah Granger and her seamstress, Margaret Cooke prime among them, decided that the women needed to unite in an organization, that they might do the work required of them, help all the needy in Nauvoo, and do much good. They asked Eliza R. Snow to write a formal constitution and by-laws to be submitted to the Prophet. But as soon as Joseph learned of their efforts, he responded: "This is not what you want. Tell the sisters their offering is accepted of the Lord, and he has something better for them than a written Constitution. I invite them all to meet with me and a few of the brethren in the Masonic Hall over my store next Thursday afternoon, and I will organize the women under the priesthood after the pattern of the priesthood . . . the Church was never perfectly organized until the women were thus organized."[16]

Emma was elected the first president of what the sisters called The Female Relief Society, Joseph saying, interestingly, that "she was ordained at the time the revelation was given to her."[17]

Emma magnified this opportunity and responsibility from the first. She spoke with great conviction and power to the sisters, and set "a threefold-theme of Unity, Purity and Charity."[18] She urged them to watch their tongues and avoid gossip, and to "throw a cloak of charity over faults that might be apparent . . . instead of criticizing, to forgive."[19]

She set an example for the others. She had always set such an example, learning from Lucy Smith, and striving to care for the Saints, she and Joseph together, and she alone during the many times when he was not able to be with her. The sick, the poor, the orphans, and widows always received of her store, no matter how scanty it might be, and of her tender encouragement and love.

As one sister said of Emma, many others did as well: "Sister Emma was benevolent and hospitable; she drew around her a large circle of friends, who were like good comrades. She was motherly in her nature to young people, always had a houseful to entertain or to be entertained."[20]

Amazing things continued to occur during the last two or three years of Joseph's life, and there were good times as well as bad. There were always socials and sing-alongs, and Nauvoo boasted a theatre for dramatic productions. Riding out with friends was a popular pastime, and even working together was a warm and comradely activity.

And the beehive of activity continued. Joseph was seeing to the publication of his translation of Abraham at the same time that John C. Bennett was beginning to teach false doctrine. Joseph was continually going into hiding, sometimes at a moment's notice. Emma wrote a long and eloquent appeal to the governor of the state, but no help was offered, no sympathy expressed. The Nauvoo Charter was threatened and changed, so that the Saints would have fewer powers and protections. On May 28, 1843, Emma was sealed to Joseph for time and all eternity, in the new and everlasting covenant which had been revealed.

In August of 1843 they moved at last into the very lovely home, later referred to as the Mansion House. "In the seventeen years of Joseph and Emma's marriage, they moved sixteen times, and perhaps only three or four times lived in a house of their own."[21] As the year 1844 began, Joseph declared himself a candidate for the presidency of the United States. This impacted Emma's life, creating much work, tension, and uncertainty. He did, interestingly, create much interest and respect and even support from powerful people in the East.

But the whirlwind of the will of God took precedence. In March Joseph organized the Quorum of Twelve Apostles, giving them the necessary keys and rolling off the kingdom from his shoulders onto theirs. On June 7 the *Nauvoo Expositior* issued heinous lies and gross untruths, and when the city council destroyed their press on June 10, the enemies of the Prophet moved in.

On June 24 Joseph and Hyrum were taken to Carthage. On June 27 they were attacked by a large mob, and suffered a martyr's death.

For all intents and purposes, Emma's life also ended. But she was pregnant and had her little clutch of children to care for. "My husband was my crown!" Emma cried out, kneeling before the dead body of her beloved Joseph. "For him and for my children I have suffered the loss of all things; and why, O God, am I thus deserted, and my bosom torn with this ten-fold anguish."[22]

Emma did not go with Brigham Young and the body of the Saints to Utah. She rented out the Mansion House for a season and moved back to the Old Homestead where her baby son, David Hyrum, was born on November 17. Save for a short season, Emma lived out her life in Nauvoo, with Lucy, Joseph's mother, staying for most of the time in the Mansion House with her. She married Lewis C. Bidamon, a non-Mormon member of the Illinois militia, who helped protect the Saints as they were preparing to leave Nauvoo. They were married from 1847–79, and the ceremony, performed by a Methodist circuit rider, took place on December,

23, 1847, which would have been Joseph's forty-second birthday. She was Bidamon's third of four wives.

Emma's life was not easy, and only her Father in Heaven could have known her continuing service, patience, disappointments, and loneliness.

The tender tribute Lucy paid Emma, while the Saints were first settling Kirtland, is the most fitting with which to end any consideration of Emma's life:

> Emma's health at this time was quite delicate, yet she did not favor herself on this account, but whatever her hands found to do she did with her might, until so far beyond her strength that she brought upon herself a heavy fit of sickness, which lasted four weeks.
>
> And, although her strength was exhausted, still her spirits were the same, which, in fact, was always the case with her, even under the most trying circumstances.
>
> I have never seen a woman in my life, who would endure every species of fatigue and hardship, from month to month, and from year to year, with that unflinching courage, zeal, and patience, which she has ever done; for I know that which she had to endure—she has been tossed upon the ocean of uncertainty—she has breasted the storms of persecution, and buffeted the rage of men and devils, which would have borne down almost any other woman. It may be, that many may yet have to encounter the same—I pray God, that this may not be the case; but, should it be, may they have grace given them according to their day, even as has been the case with her.[23]

ENDNOTES

1. Smith, *History of Joseph Smith*, 126.
2. Staker, *Women of Faith*, vol. 1, 343.
3. "Ten Things You Don't Know About Emma Smith," ChurchofJesusChrist.org.
4. Turley, *Women of Faith*, 349.
5. Ibid., 350.
6. Jones, 14.
7. Ibid., 15.
8. Ibid.
9. Joseph Smith, *History of the Church*, 1:88–89.
10. Jones, 85.
11. Ibid., 87.
12. Toone "The New Joseph Smith Papers volume shows the Mormon prophet's 'toughness'," *Deseret News*, Sept. 27, 2017.
13. Joseph Smith, *History of the Church*, III:250.

14. Jones, 92–93.

15. Ibid., 101.

16. Kimball, autobiography, 51; as quoted in Women of Faith, 119.

17. Jones, *Emma's Glory and Sacrifice,* 118.

18. Ibid., 119.

19. Ibid.

20. *Woman's Exponent* as quoted in *Emma's Glory,* 119.

21. Smith, *History of Joseph Smith,* note 5, end of chapter 37.

22. Jones, 158.

23. Smith, *History of Joseph Smith,* note 5, 248–49.

MARY MUSSELMAN WHITMER

MARY MUSSELMAN WAS BORN ON August 27, 1778, in Germany. She immigrated to the United States, but we do not know when. She married Peter Whitmer, who was a Pennsylvania farmer and of German descent, which must have pleased her.

Mary and Peter moved to New York and purchased a farm in the area of Fayette. All their energies were bent upon making the farm work and produce. Some sources say they were strict members of the Presbyterian Church; others of the German Reformed Church. Mary had given birth to eight children, five sons and three daughters. Eventually five of her sons would become witnesses to the truth of the Book of Mormon and sign their names to be read and recorded for all generations to come. Her daughter Catherine married Hiram Page, who was also one of the witnesses, and Elizabeth Whitmer married Oliver Cowdery, one of the prime witnesses of the Book of Mormon.

Before this occurred, the plates needed to be translated, and the book to be published, and become a reality!

It was actually Lucy Mack Smith who first met members of the Whitmer family. But it is most singularly amazing how this association progressed. Joseph and Oliver Cowdery were in Pennsylvania, one hundred and fifty miles from Fayette, working on the translation of the plates. Lucy Mack Smith records:

> One morning as (Joseph) applied the Urim and Thummim to his eyes to look upon the record, instead of the words of the book being given to him, he was commanded to write a letter to one David Whitmer, who lived in Waterloo. This man Joseph had never seen, but he was instructed to say to him that he must come with his team immediately,

in order to convey Joseph and Oliver back to his house, that they might remain with him there until the translation should be completed, as an evil-designing people were seeking to take away Joseph's life in order to prevent the work of God from going forth among the world.[1]

Joseph wrote the letter and sent it off. When David Whitmer showed it to his family, they were somewhat astonished. His father reminded him that he had sowed wheat which he must harrow on the next day. Then he was to spread plaster on needed areas of his land. In other words, he could not just run off to parts unknown for reasons that seemed remarkable and strange.

However, David prayed and asked the Lord for a testimony that he should go. The voice of the Spirit told him to harrow his wheat and then go to Pennsylvania. But there were at least two days' solid work before him, so he prayed again that he might be able to do the work more quickly than usual.

He did not divide the land as was customary, but drove round and round it and discovered by dinnertime that he had harrowed half of the field. By evening he had finished the whole two days' work.

"When he informed his father of the fact, he replied, 'Well, there must be some overruling power in this thing, and I think you had better go as soon as you get your plaster of paris sown and bring up the man with his scribe.'"[2]

But the following morning three unknown men had come into the field and sown the plaster so quickly that even the children noticed their speed, and the family surmised, with astonishment, that there were supernatural powers at work here.

Joseph and Oliver rode with David to upstate New York, leaving Emma behind for the time being, though in a short while she was able to join them.

These were the conditions under which Mary Whitmer was burdened with three long-entrenched house guests staying free of charge in her small cabin that was one and a half stories in size.

She was entirely aware of the extraordinary circumstances, as Joseph and Oliver worked long hours translating with the strange mechanism Joseph wore, and writing the words which flowed miraculously from the young Prophet's lips.

Yet life, daily life, went on. Nothing is written of Emma's time there, but knowing what we do of her we can easily assume that she was a help

34

to the older woman. Mary was in her forties at this time, so she was not young, and she was not old. But her men were busy every minute of the day with the work of the farm and the care of the animals. Mary's work in the house—baking, cooking, cleaning, seeing to laundry, gardening, and perhaps looking after chicken or geese—began early and went as late as it took to get it all completed.

This particular evening she was going out to milk the cows—the last chore of a long day's labor. As she went "she met a stranger carrying something on his back that looked like a knapsack. At first she was a little afraid of him, but when he spoke to her in a kind, friendly tone and began to explain to her the nature of the work which was going on in her house, *she was filled with inexpressible joy and satisfaction.* He then untied his knapsack and showed her a bundle of plates, which in size and appearance corresponded with the description subsequently given by the witnesses to the Book of Mormon. This strange person turned the leaves of the book of plates over, leaf after leaf, and also showed her the engravings upon them; after which he told her to be patient and faithful in bearing her burden a little longer, promising that if she would do so, she should be blessed; and her reward would be sure, if she proved faithful to the end.

"The personage then suddenly vanished with the plates, and where he went, she could not tell."[3]

David Whitmer added to the account, the following words that the kindly messenger said: "You have been very faithful and diligent in your labors, but you are very tired because of the increase of your toil; it is proper therefore that you should receive a witness that your faith may be strengthened."

Mary's grandson, John C. Whitmer, wrote: "From that moment my grandmother was enabled to perform her household duties with comparative ease, and she felt no more inclination to murmur because her lot was hard. I knew my grandmother to be a good, noble and truthful woman, and I have not the least doubt of her statement in regard to seeing the plates being strictly true. She was a strong believer in the Book of Mormon until the day of her death."[4]

This took place in the year 1829. There was a change in Mary, which affected the actual work and routine of daily life in her home—but, also, I would suppose, a change in the spirit or atmosphere in those few crowded rooms.

The Lord had revealed unto the least among them a heavenly messenger, a rare and sacred experience, and a word of comfort to one of his patient, noble daughters who was serving and sustaining his own servant, Joseph Smith.

How much of this Mary understood, we do not know. But she must have realized the deeply special and remarkable events that were taking place in her home. And she must have felt loved. I think that may have been one of the purposes of the stranger's visit to her. The Book of Mormon was published and available for purchase on March 26, 1830. On April 6, according to divine command, the Church of Jesus Christ was legally and spiritually established—in Mary's humble home. The six original members, the number required by law, were Joseph Smith, Jr., Oliver Cowdery, Hyrum and Samuel Smith, and David and Peter Whitmer, Jr., Mary's sons.

We know that the Whitmer family went with the Saints to Kirtland, the new gathering place of the Church. We know that they were noble and valiant, supported by their mother, we can be sure. Indeed, the women of the Whitmer family, along with Emma Smith and possibly Thankful Pratt, made clothing for the men who were being sent on the first major mission of the Church. As Lucy Mack Smith recalled, this "was no easy task, as the most of it had to be manufactured out of the raw material."[5]

Along with Oliver Cowdery, Peter Whitmer was one of those early missionaries to Missouri. Mary's sons suffered much. They were threatened at gunpoint, and Hiram Page, her son-in-law, was severely beaten. But the persecutions did not weaken the family's faith. Peter was sick with ague and fever for four long weeks, but he speaks triumphantly of his courage in the face of the mobs. "The testimony I gave that mob made them fear and tremble, and I escaped from them."[6]

David Whitmer had brought Joseph and Oliver to his home. John Whitmer had been one of Joseph's most important scribes. Peter Jr. had assisted during the first printing of the Book of Mormon, and these young men had received special revelations from God for them. The gospel was interwoven into their very marrow.

The Whitmers went first to Jackson County, where they were promised a special, lasting inheritance in the land of Zion, due to their great faithfulness to the work. But two years later the mobs drove them from Jackson County, and they lost everything!

They then joined with Joseph and the Saints in Kirtland, Ohio. But following the wonderful spiritual manifestations at the time of the dedication of the temple, there was a sense of madness and speculation, which did not last but did much to destroy the safety, spirituality, and unity of the Church.

Then the days in Kirtland were fraught with discouragement and near-ruin, for the bank failure, which swept the whole country, had devastating effects here.

Yet, the Whitmer family remained and went with the rest of the Saints to Far West, Missouri, where the nightmares of cruelty and persecution continued and increased.

All of this came to a head in 1838 when Mary's sons David and John, as well as Oliver Cowdery, were excommunicated from the Church. There was good reason for this action being taken. But it split the strong family; it destroyed much of what they had been, what they had desired and embraced for so many hard years.

We cannot understand the physical and spiritual exhaustion that accompanied such experiences. We can easily imagine anger as well as discouragement. Had not this family given and given, and then given more? Had they not been honored of the Lord—and now to be reduced to this?

There is another vital fact that assuredly influenced Mary and tried her to the core of her being. On September 22, 1836 (and did this take place in Kirtland? We do not know) Peter Whitmer Jr., the youngest of their children, died of tuberculosis, or consumption. He was within days of turning twenty-seven years old—*and* he left a wife, Vashti, and two daughters behind him. Vashti was expecting their third child, a daughter who was born in 1837, following her father's death, and named after her mother.

Two months later Christian Whitmer, the oldest of Mary's children, died of a severe infection in his leg. He was thirty-seven years old.

This afflicted family did not go with the Saints to Nauvoo. Mother Whitmer, as she was lovingly called, had a magnificent influence upon the women of the Church. We have no idea how much she shared with weak or suffering Saints concerning the vision she had been afforded, and the Spirit of the Lord at that time—in her heart and in her home. But she worked and she loved, and she lifted and sustained many in the midst of the sufferings and changes which came to her family.

Mary went with her husband and sons to the nearby town of Richmond, Missouri. We do not know all that was in her heart, but she had no other option as a woman; as a mother and a wife.

Vashti, Peter's little widow, took her three fatherless children to Richmond, as well. Surely there must have been a tender relationship between these two women, mourning the loss of son and husband together. Vashti's father had died young, at the age of fifty-nine, and her mother was far away from her, in the east.

Mary's sons kept their testimonies of the foundation of the Church and of the truthfulness of the Book of Mormon. In 1861, white-haired and aging, David Whitmer told the young missionary Jacob Gates (who was later to marry Brigham Young's remarkable daughter Susa) that he could not agree with polygamy, but he knew the Book of Mormon was true and that "Joseph Smith was a true Prophet . . . that Brigham Young was carrying out the principles that Joseph taught before he was martyred."[7]

But now life went on peacefully and normally, without the trauma, fear, and loss that had accompanied their years in the Church. Did Mary miss it at times? Did she wonder and yearn for her friends, for the fierce loyalty and courage which had been theirs as they participated in such stirring events?

John actually stayed in Far West, "a city that vanished and left him with an isolated farm."[8] David established a successful livery stable and transportation business in Richmond.

Peter Whitmer Sr. died in 1854, and Mary followed him in 1856. Their son Jacob also died in 1856, and Mary's son-in-law, Hiram Page, died in 1852. His widow, Mary's daughter Catherine, lived with her son just outside Richmond until at least 1880.

Mary's daughter Elizabeth went with her husband, Oliver Cowdery, until in 1848 he was reconciled to the LDS Church. Sadly, he died only two years later of a lung condition. After that, Elizabeth lived with her daughter, Maria, who had married a Dr. Charles Johnson. An interesting portrait remains of her, in the words of a Mr. William Lang, a prominent Ohio attorney, who worked with Oliver Cowdery for years. He called her "a beautiful woman, whose quiet nature, sweet temper, and kind disposition, won her friends wherever she was known."[9]

Vashti, who had raised her daughters and lived alone since Peter's death in 1836, lived until April of 1882, dying at seventy-five, nearly fifty years after her husband. Perhaps she was the longest lived of this remarkable family.

The early Church would not have proceeded without the Whitmer family. Their loving contributions cannot be measured. As Richard Anderson put it, "This was a family that nourished the Church."[10]

And Mary, as Mother, stood from the beginning at the quiet heart of the work.

ENDNOTES

1. Smith, *History of Joseph Smith*, 192.
2. Ibid., 193.
3. "Mary Musselman Whitmer," *LDS Women's History*, ldswomenshistory.blogspot.com/2008/03/mary-musselman-whitmer.html.
4. "Emma Smith & Mary Whitmer Witnesses to the Gold Plates," *Book of Mormon Evidence*, bookofmormonevidence.org/emma-smith-mary-whitmer-witnesses-to-the-gold-plates/.
5. Smith, *Biographical Sketches*, 169.
6. Anderson, "The Whitmers: A Family That Nourished the Church," churchofjesuschrist.org/study/ensign/1979/08.
7. Anderson, ibid.
8. Anderson, ibid.
9. Anderson, ibid.
10. Anderson, ibid.

KIRTLAND, OHIO

Kirtland was a sleepy little town until the Mormons descended upon it. Joseph and Emma arrived February 1, 1831, at Newel K. Whitney's store. Joseph greeted Newel with warm enthusiasm and said, "Well, you have prayed me here. So what do you want to do with me?" Edward Partridge was called as bishop three days after Joseph's arrival, and the Saints flooded into the city, more than tripling the population by 1838.

The first temple of this dispensation was begun in 1833 and dedicated March 27, 1836. Joseph's Lectures on Faith were presented in the printing office, and the first edition of the Doctrine and Covenants and the second of the Book of Mormon were printed there.

The Savior himself appeared to accept the temple. Moses, Elias, and Elijah appeared and restored priesthood keys. Many revelations now in the Doctrine and Covenants were given to Joseph Smith there, and the School of the Prophets was held in this sacred house.

Following this period of spiritual enlightenment and joy, there came a spirit of discord, criticism, and greed. With the bank failure of 1837, many suffered and lost their jobs, their investments, and even their homes. There was a spirit of dissension and such cruel criticism against the Prophet that he was forced to flee. Soon after, the body of the Church abandoned Kirtland. By mid-July 1838 more than 1,600 had left, leaving their beautiful, sacred temple behind.

MARY FIELDING SMITH

DURING ALL HER GROWING UP and maturing years, Mary Fielding lived in the small town of Honidon, England, where she had been born. She learned from her parents how to work hard, and she learned to believe in God and reverence him, much as Joseph and Hyrum Smith had been taught by their mother to do.

She was born July 21, 1801, and we wonder what her thoughts were when she bade goodbye to her brother, Joseph, and her sister, Mercy, who emigrated to Canada in 1832. Their parents had been farmers, and they wished to establish farms of their own. Two years later, Mary joined them, indicating that they were meeting with success and were pleased with their circumstances in Canada. In 1834 Joseph was thirty-seven years old, Mercy twenty-seven years old, and Mary thirty-six.

The three siblings lived together and became part of a little group that was a break-off from the Methodist religion. When a stranger arrived in their area, preaching a new and rather strange religion, he was coldly received. But the stranger, Parley P. Pratt, was a gifted preacher and teacher, and persuaded his friend, John Taylor, who was not even baptized yet, to join him on a preaching tour. Outside the large city of Toronto stood many farms, but the two men happened upon the farm of Joseph Fielding.

Frightened and a bit intimidated, Mary and Mercy slipped away to the home of a neighbor. Joseph told the strangers, "We do not want a new revelation or a new religion contrary to the Bible."

With a smile Parley Pratt responded, "If that is all, we shall soon remove your prejudices."

This marked the beginning—and the end. The missionaries urged Joseph Fielding to send for his sisters, and all three, with their intelligent minds and open spirits, were converted, and baptized on May 21, 1836. At the same time their friends, Leonora and John Taylor, were baptized.

The pace of their lives moved quickly after that. By the spring of 1837 they had gathered to Kirtland, Ohio, where most of the Saints resided. But in the summer Joseph and Heber C. Kimball were called on a mission to England, and Mary's big sister, along with her husband, Robert B. Thompson, returned to Canada on a mission as well. Suddenly Mary was on her own, and she felt the loneliness of it.

We get two vital insights into Mary's soul from this first challenging period of her life—insights that indicate a strength of character and spirit, a dedication, and a faith that remained with her, and were strengthened, throughout the rest of her life.

In a letter to Mercy she wrote: "I feel more and more convinced that it is through suffering that we are to be made perfect, and I have already found it to have the effect of driving me nearer to the Lord and so suffering has become a great blessing to me."[1]

The second insight concerns the Prophet Joseph and his brother, the man who was soon to become her husband, her eternal mate. She speaks of attending a Sabbath-day meeting in the beauty of the new temple and gazing upon Joseph and his brethren as they sat in the Melchizedek Priesthood pulpits. She wrote in another letter: "All, I believe, (are) faithful servants of the Living God. Joseph and Hyrum I know best and love much. While I looked at them, my heart was drawn out in earnest prayer to our Heavenly Father in their behalf, *and also for the prophetess, their aged mother, whose eyes are frequently bathed in tears when she looks at or speaks of them.*"[2]

In October, near the end of 1837, Hyrum's wife, Jerusha, died, leaving her five children motherless. Hyrum was beside himself with grief. Joseph, with concern for the suffering of this beloved brother, went to the Lord, who instructed him to ask Mary Fielding to be Hyrum's wife.

Marriage had always been a solemn matter to Mary. Perhaps because she knew a revelation had come from the Lord himself, she had courage to face all the unknowns in this sudden challenge. Moreover, she had always said she did not think she would do very well as a step-mother.

But she personally sought the will of the Lord for her life, and on the day before Christmas she and Hyrum were wed. Mary was thirty-six years old, Hyrum less than two months away from thirty-eight.

Due to the nation-wide Bank Panic of 1837, and the madness of speculation that consumed the Saints, a spirit of apostasy swept through the Church, and persecution of the Prophet Joseph became so severe that in January 1838 he left Kirtland.

In the first seven months of the year, more than sixteen hundred Saints fled the city, heading for Far West, Missouri—a daunting journey of nine hundred miles! Converts were still arriving from overseas, and the city's population tripled by May 1838.

But the mobs were further incited by their success in driving the Mormons from their homes in Jackson County. As the mobsters went to the extremity of burning their own homes and blaming it on the Latter-day Saints, Governor Boggs felt justified and issued the infamous Extermination Order: "The Mormons must be treated as enemies and must be exterminated or driven from the state."

Under the terrifying madness of these conditions, Mary, now pregnant with her first child, watched the mobs encircle Far West, emboldened to take Joseph and others, including Hyrum, as prisoners.

Joseph Sr. and Lucy Mack Smith were horrified and weakened by the cry of men, who were like wild, possessed animals, literally hungering for the blood of Joseph and Hyrum. Lucy wrote with power and anguish about this, but we have no record in words of all Emma and Mary likewise suffered.

Joseph and Hyrum were not killed, but they were dragged off to prison and a still-unknown fate, while Mary lay helpless, awaiting the birth of her son.

Joseph Fielding Smith survived his birth, but it was the care and nursing of his aunt Mercy that secured his life, and Mary's, too. Mary somehow marshalled the strength to visit Hyrum in his dungeon prison in Liberty, Missouri, and he had the joy of seeing his newly born son. When the Saints, under conditions of great hardship, abandoned the state, Mary wrote a vivid description of her own sufferings to her brother, Joseph Fielding, serving a mission in England:

> Shortly after his birth I took a severe cold, which brought on chills and fever; this, together with the anxiety of mind I had to endure, threatened to bring me to the gates of death. *I was at least four months entirely unable to take any care either of myself or child;* but the Lord was merciful in so ordering things that my dear sister could be with me. Her child was five months old when mine was born; so she had strength given her to

nurse them both . . . I had to be removed more than two hundred miles, chiefly on my bed. I suffered much during that journey.[3]

Mary reached Quincy, Illinois, where Hyrum was able to join her in April 1839, after four long months in prison.

Her spirit, vital with joy and faith, can be felt in the following words from the same letter as quoted above: "We are now living in Commerce, on the bank of the great Mississippi river. The situation is very pleasant; you would be much pleased to see it. How long we may be permitted to enjoy it I know not; but the Lord knows what is best for us. I feel but little concerned about where I am, if I can keep my mind staid upon God; for, you know in this there is perfect peace. I believe the Lord is overruling all things for our good. I suppose our enemies look upon us with astonishment and disappointment."[4]

By 1840 the city of Nauvoo was perfectly organized, and missionaries were being sent to all parts of the world. New revelations continued to come, and new European converts. But in September of that year Joseph Sr. died at the age of sixty-nine, and this was a terrible blow to Lucy and to all of his sons. Mercy's husband, Robert B. Thompson, delivered the funeral oration.

Less than a year later, in August 1841, Don Carlos Smith and Robert, who had worked together on the *Times and Seasons*, died unexpectedly from tuberculosis, due to the unhealthy conditions in which they worked. Don Carlos Smith had been made president of the high priests when only nineteen, and he stood six feet four inches tall, with a commanding presence, like his brothers. Brother Robinson said of him, "I do think he was one of the most perfect men I ever saw."

Robert had been made the official Church historian and, among other things, was a colonel in the Nauvoo Legion. He was also the husband of Mary's sister, Mercy.[5]

There was no peace for the Prophet Joseph during all this time, and the troubles often spilled over onto Hyrum, who would still do anything in his power to protect his brother.

There had been so many times of danger and impending harm. But when the *Nauvoo Expositor*, one issue only on June 7, 1844, was declared, with horror, a public nuisance, the enemies of the Prophet jumped at their chance. The two brothers had sought refuge across the Mississippi River, in hopes of arranging some place in the West for the Saints to go. But when Joseph returned to Nauvoo, his brother Hyrum went with him.

Joseph was reconciled to death, but he wanted Hyrum to outlive him and to lead the Church. This is when he made the remarkable statement about this man whom Mary had come to love with all of her being: "I could pray in my heart that all my brethren were like unto my beloved brother, Hyrum, who possesses the mildness of a lamb, the integrity of a Job, and, in short, the meekness and humility of Christ; and I love him with that love that is stronger than death."[6]

The brothers surrendered themselves and were taken to nearby Carthage. Imprisoned in the small jailhouse, they knew their deaths were imminent. Shortly after five p.m. on June 27, more than a hundred men, with faces painted black and grotesque, surrounded the jail, crowded the narrow stairway, and forced the door.

The men inside had very little with them as means of defense. Hyrum, at the left of the door, trying to parry the guns with his cane, stood in direct line of the gunfire. He was the first to be hit and the first to fall. He cried, "I am a dead man!" Joseph called out, "Oh, dear brother Hyrum!"

The details of their last days and their deaths, and the nobility of the Saints in Nauvoo who accepted with faith and long-suffering the slaying of the prophets, is a story for the generations of eternity to honor and hold close.

But Mary, mortal woman, was bereft of the noble husband she cherished, and left alone in an unkind, uncaring world. As she knelt beside Hyrum she cried out to him, finding it impossible to accept that he lay dead in her arms. Her daughter Martha Ann recorded: "How sad and sorrowful my darling mother used to look. She scarcely ever smiled again. If we could get her to laugh, we thought we had accomplished quite a feat."[7]

That same autumn of 1844 Heber C. Kimball took Mary as one of his plural wives that he might at least look after her welfare from time to time. Brigham was one of the first to leave Nauvoo in February 1846. Mary was determined to make ready. What it cost her in pain, in courage—in anguish for Lucy Mack Smith, and the family of the Prophet and Patriarch who would be left behind—is really incomprehensible to us. But she knew where her happiness lay and what Hyrum would have expected of her. I like to think of the tender farewell between the two women, mother and wife, and of Lucy's parting blessing upon the head of her noble daughter-in-law.

Again, in the words of Martha Ann:

We left our home just as it was—our furniture and the fruit trees hanging full of rosy-cheeked peaches. We bid goodbye to the loved home that reminded us of our father everywhere we turned. I was five years old when we started from Nauvoo. We crossed over the Mississippi in the skiff in the dusk of evening. We bid goodbye to our dear, old, feeble grandmother (Lucy Mack Smith). I can never forget the bitter tears she shed when she bid us goodbye for the last time in this life. She knew it would be the last time she would see her son's family.[8]

Mary proved herself, even during the early Winter Quarter days when she traveled to St. Joseph with her brother and son for needed supplies. During the night it seemed her team had wandered off and, though the wide prairie was open to them, they could see the animals nowhere. Both Josephs went in search of the beasts, through the tall wet grass, and returned soaked and discouraged, but without the cattle. They found Mary on her knees, entreating the Lord. As the men took breakfast, she walked purposefully out of camp—ignored the misinformation given by the driver of the large herd of beef cattle nearby, and found her two cows secured to a clump of willows by a somewhat hidden creek.[9]

This kind of faith was exhibited time after time, including the famous healing of her sick cow when Captain Lott, under whom her little group had been placed, treated her unkindly, even despitefully, letting her know she was nothing but a burden to him, and should have returned instead of placing this burden on him. (And do our hearts wonder what Hyrum was feeling and thinking as he watched from his vantage point?)

Lott was sure he was right when one of Mary's oxen lay down and appeared to be dying. But she quietly retrieved a bottle of consecrated oil and asked her brother and James Lawson to anoint and administer to the beast. They made no objections, and the animal stirred, rose, and moved off, seeming in fine fettle—and, with the others, bringing Mary to the valley many hours before Captain Lott and the rest!

Even coming into the Salt Lake Valley, Mary had ideas of her own. The brethren had expected her to select property at the center of the city, but she rode Hyrum's old horse out and away until she found land near some springs in what is now East Millcreek. Here she carved a homestead for herself and her family, in what was then virgin land. First came a house and a dugout barn, then the hard work of cultivating forty acres.

The work—and the challenging years that preceded it—took their toll. When Mary became ill, the Kimballs took her in and nursed her, but she died on September 21, 1852, at the young age of fifty-one. Martha Ann was only eleven, and Joseph F. was about to turn fourteen.

Heber C. Kimball said at her funeral: "If any person has lived the life of a saint, she has. If any person has acted the part of a mother, she has. . . . I have never seen a person in my life that had a greater desire to live than she had, and there was only one thing she desired to live for, and that was to see her family."[10]

Her son, Joseph F. who had passed through so many trials and hardships at her side, paid a most tender, remarkable tribute to her: "How I love and cherish true Motherhood! Nothing beneath the Celestial kingdom can surpass my deathless love for the sweet, true, noble soul who gave me birth—my own, own mother! O she was good! She was true! She was pure! She was indeed a Saint! A royal daughter of God! To her I owe my very existence, as also my success in life, coupled with the favor and mercy of God!"[11]

ENDNOTES

1. Rawson, "The Indomitable Faith of Mary Fielding Smith."
2. Ibid.
3. Madsen, *In Their Own Words*, 99.
4. Ibid.
5. McCloud, *Photobiography*, 102.
6. Ibid., 130.
7. Rawson, ibid.
8. Ibid.
9. "Mary Fielding Prayers to Find Her Lost Oxen," *LDS Scripture Teachings*, ldsscriptureteachings.org/2015/08/20/mary-fielding-smith-prays-to-find-her-lost-oxen/.
10. Rawson, ibid.
11. Rawson, ibid.

ELIZA ROXY SNOW

OF ALL THE THINGS ELIZA R. Snow aspired to, of all the qualities of mind and spirit which she developed, she was at heart, at her very core, a poet. She was born on January 21, 1804, in Beckett, Massachusetts, though the family moved the following year to Mantua, Ohio. She had three sisters and three brothers, and book learning, and a seriousness about studying and learning were part of the training they received. At an early age Eliza worked in her father's office, but she also learned housekeeping skills from her mother. Her first poem was published in 1825.[1] And this expression of the soul of a poet was to become one of the major ways in which she would contribute to the kingdom, and a key part of the strength by which she would endure her hardships.

When Joseph Smith visited the Snow home in the winter of 1830–31, Eliza's mother and older sister, Rosetta, both accepted the gospel message and were baptized by the Prophet, himself. But Eliza, in much the same fashion as Brigham Young, studied carefully and pondered what she had heard. Four years later, in April 1835, she was baptized. Her confirmation was such a deeply spiritual experience that it sustained her throughout her life. Of it she said, "I saw a beautiful candle with an unusual long, bright blaze directly over my feet. I sought to know the interpretation, and received the following, 'The lamp of intelligence shall be lighted over your path.' I was satisfied."[2]

But she also remembered that during her period of questioning and hesitating she had promised the Lord, in her prayers, that if she ever learned that this work were true, she would praise his name, and so she did throughout the remainder of her life.[3]

In December, Eliza traveled to Kirtland and was there for the dedication of the first temple of the dispensation of the fulness of times. Here, also, she taught school, boarding with the Prophet and his family.

After a brief visit home in which she tucked her childhood away forever, Eliza returned to Kirtland. She speaks in her personal history of donating to the temple fund and being ceded a city lot. She speaks of her fears concerning her beloved brother, Lorenzo, who was attending a Presbyterian college and was not interested in the gospel. However, he came to spend his vacation with her sister and herself, studied Hebrew and the doctrines of the kingdom, was baptized, and became a mighty leader in the kingdom.

Eliza speaks of being present at the dedication of the Kirtland Temple but says nothing of the wondrous spiritual visitations and manifestations that took place, nor of the terrible apostasy and speculation that ensued.

But her family left Kirtland, with Illinois as their destination, though they went via Adam-ondi-Ahman, and then Far West. Before leaving Missouri and reaching their destination, she does state calmly: "We could not decide which was most to be dreaded, the Militia or the mob—no property was safe within the reach of either."[4]

She does speak of the rain turning to snow, the tent frozen and needing to be thawed, the terrible mud, the stress on the teams—and the kindness of "an elderly gentleman on horseback (who) overtook us, and, after riding alongside for some time, apparently absorbed in deep thought," inquired who they were and why they were all traipsing alongside the tired team, and, learning somewhat of their circumstances, emphatically remarked, "If I were in your places, I should want the Governor of the State hitched at the head of my teams."[5]

Eliza's experiences in Far West were ones of great pain and suffering, though she makes no reference to the worst of what she suffered there.

Not until early March did they leave and start once more for Illinois, arriving in Quincy, where many of the exiled Saints were already temporarily living. Of her journey she does give some sobering examples, such as the night her family spent in a small log structure with about eighty other refugees. They could not get warm, despite the crowded conditions, and all their food froze and could not be thawed despite a blazing fire. Yet she speaks of the cheerful attempts of the sufferers and the lack of discouragement or complaining.

She had only temporary homes and temporary comfort, though she and her mother were able to earn somewhat of a living through their sewing and tailoring skills, and the kindness of the family with which they lived. And yet, for nearly three years, from January 1836 to about October 1838, Eliza's muse was silent; she wrote no poetry, no expressions of beauty that spoke through the poetry of her heart. The demands of reality, which included anguish and incredulity as well as suffering, had silenced for a time the voice from within.

Commerce, where the Saints gathered, stretched along a wide bend of the Mississippi River. After the prophet returned from captivity, he renamed the old settlement Nauvoo—meaning a lovely situation or a beautiful place. Here Eliza, along with the other Saints, found what seemed a stationary home and a place where their united efforts could bring comfort, progress, and joy.

Eliza always served with a will, but she seldom recorded the details of her contributions. She was again writing poetry and, though imperfect, her verses were a passionate history of what the Saints and she, herself, were experiencing.

Some of her poems she wrote in the form of psalms. I quote from one entitled "Psalm No. 2," which was published in the *Times and Seasons,* 1 September 1841:

> Let the saints lift up their voice—let them not keep silence—let them declare in the ears of this generation; what the Lord has done for his persecuted people.
>
> Let them speak of his mercy and his goodness—let them proclaim his wisdom and his power, in delivering them from the hands of their enemies.
>
> . . . When we had fallen low beneath the weight of oppression, and had well nigh become a prey to those that thirsted for our blood! Then the Lord heard our supplications, and the Most High wrought a way for our deliverance . . .
>
> The Lord hath done it—let his name be exalted—let his faithfulness be declared in the congregations of the people—let his statutes be kept in continual remembrance by all who profess to be his saints."[6]

The Prophet Joseph himself gave her the unique calling as Zion's Poetess, to represent the people of the Lord through the music of words, the beauty of verse.

In the sketch of her life Eliza wrote: "To narrate what transpired within the seven years in which we built and occupied Nauvoo, the beautiful, would fill many volumes. . . . Some of the most important events of my life transpired within that brief term."[7]

One of the things that transpired in Nauvoo was the organization of the Female Relief Society of Nauvoo, encouraged by Sisters Sarah M. Cleveland and Elizabeth Ann Whitney. The women had met to form an organization, and the Prophet told them that the document Eliza had written up for their constitution was the best he had seen, but the Lord had in mind "something better"; the Prophet wished to organize them "after the pattern, or order, of the Priesthood."[8]

Every spiritual aspect, every priesthood power, every authority is done with the proper priesthood keys. On April 28, 1842, Joseph told the women, "I now turn the key to you in the name of God, and this Society shall rejoice and knowledge and intelligence shall flow down from this time."[9]

This organization, and the promises and powers embodied therein, were to play a vastly important part in Eliza Snow's life.

In Nauvoo Eliza was sealed to the Prophet Joseph Smith under the celestial law of marriage, and she testified of the purity of the principle and its power for growth and for righteousness in the lives of both women and men.

Eliza was involved with her family, with her own efforts to earn her living and keep, with the affairs of the Relief Society, of which she was the official secretary. There was a constant need for service, as new converts poured into the city by the thousands, and every moment seemed filled with something of interest or of good.

There were, of course, the ever-present threats and dangers to the Prophet Joseph. Eliza was deeply aware of these and wrote many a verse of praise, or support, and expressing her testimony of the Prophet—and there were some poems of righteous anger against the vicious and unholy men who wished Joseph Smith's death.

When Joseph and Hyrum were martyred in Carthage, Eliza felt the loss and horror deeply. She wrote: "The awful tragedy of the 27th of June 1844 is a livid, burning, scathing stain on our national escutcheon. To look upon the noble, lifeless forms of those brothers, Joseph and Hyrum Smith . . . slaughtered in their manhood and in their innocence . . . what it was for loving wives and children, the loyal heart may feel, but let language keep silence!"[10]

Change; constant change, and with it never slackening uncertainty, and an awareness of danger and the designs of the Saints' enemies. While preparing for a mass departure, life still had to go on. Eliza taught a school with sixty-five students, went for a time to stay with her parents in Walnut Grove some miles from Nauvoo, and officiated in the temple during her final months in the beloved City of Joseph.

On October 3, 1844, Eliza became one of the plural wives of Brigham Young. Throughout their long and varied associations, she never took his name but always went by Eliza R. Snow, or sometimes Smith. After his death, she did use the surname of the Prophet Joseph more often.

In October 1845, another significant thing happened in Eliza's life: she wrote her last of nearly one hundred poems composed in Nauvoo. This, perhaps influenced by conversations with Joseph or with Zina, would become her most powerful, poetic, spiritual contribution to the kingdom. In the third verse she touches on a tender, eternal truth, which has been of comfort to many hearts. In verse four she writes: "In the heavens are parents single? No, the thought makes reason stare; Truth is reason—truth eternal Tells me I've a mother there."

She had been staying, or boarding, with the family of Stephen Markham, so with them crossed the Mississippi on a ferry boat to begin her own journey. The date was February 13, 1846. For several days, Eliza records in her journal, there were snowstorms and intense cold. But the Saints were well organized and cheerful, and the men would remove the snow, pitch tents, and build a home-like atmosphere. When the Nauvoo Band came into camp there was music and a sense of celebration for all.

Eliza wrote many "traveling" poems during the exodus from Nauvoo. One particularly loved and encouraging is the following, entitled "Camp of Israel":

> Lo! a mighty host of people
> Tented on the western shore
> Of the noble Mississippi
> They for weeks were crossing o'er.
>
> At the last day's dawn of winter,
> Bound with frost & wrapt in snow,
> Hark! The sound is onward, onward!
> Camp of Israel! Rise and go.
>
> All at once is life in motion—
> Trunks and beds & baggage fly;
> Oxen yok'd & horses harness'd—

Tents roll'd up, are passing by.
Soon the carriage wheels are rolling—
Onward to a woodland dell,
Where at sunset all are quarter'd—
Camp of Israel! All is well.

Thickly round, the tents are cluster'd
Neighb'rilng folk together blend—
Supper serv'd—the hymns are chanted—
And the evening pray'rs ascend.
Last of all the guards are station'd—
Heavn'ns! Must guards be serving here?
Who would harm these homeless exiles?
Camp of Israel! Never fear.

Where is freedom? where is justice?
Both have from this nation fled;
And the blood of martyr'd prophets
Must be answer'd on its head!

Therefore to your tents, O Jacob!
Like our father Abra'm dwell –
God will execute his purpose -
Camp of Israel! all is well.[11]

Her journal of the journey to the Great Salt Lake is more delightfully thorough and complete than her personal writings beforehand, and it contains many verses written for her friends. When there was a need, Eliza filled it with verse!

During the long days at Winter Quarters, waiting to move on, Eliza had learned that her mother had died. Though saddened, Eliza took comfort knowing she was safe now and free from the ills she had suffered in life.

During this period Eliza also established a warm closeness with some of Brigham Young's other wives, so that a "family feeling" began to develop among them.

On April 8, 1847, Eliza records: "Elder Kimball was passing my 'study' to day when I told him, as I was number'd among his children, I wished to know if he would acknowledge me as one. He said he would & I told him that I should claim a father's blessing. He said he would give me one. I asked when? to which he replied 'now.' I told him I was ready; he said to me then, 'A father's blessing shall rest upon you from this time forth.' From this time I call him father."[12]

Eliza was in need of love, tenderness, and a true sense of belonging. After arriving in the Valley, this was developed, and at length, attained within the large and versatile family of President Young. She enjoyed a favored place in his household, and all gave her a certain deference and respect.

Her Salt Lake days became consumed with service, culminating in 1867 when Brigham appointed her to re-establish the Women's Relief Society, not only in the Salt Lake Valley but through all the valleys of the mountains, throughout all the Church. She was sixty-three years old, seasoned and ready. Two years later he asked her to also organize an association for the young women, and at length she became involved in effecting the same for the children. She and Zina D. Young, a sister wife, organized more than thirty Primaries throughout the valleys.

The light of Eliza's faith and the scope of her experience were so powerful that the sisters, and even the brethren, of the Church responded to her, and were moved to change and improve. She was a compelling speaker, and now she became more powerful than ever, visiting wards throughout the Utah Territory, tirelessly giving of herself, firing up the courage and righteous desires of her listeners. The bishops, as well as the women leaders, enjoyed working with her. Her manner was forthright, allowing no weakness of minor excuses or complaints. In Lehi, Utah, in October of 1869, she told the sisters: "We want to be ladies in very deed, not according to the term of the word as the world judges, but fit companions of the gods and holy ones. We have got to cooperate not only with our husbands but with God. . . . I know we like to be appreciated but if we do not get all the appreciation which we think is our due, what matters? We know the Lord's laid high responsibility upon us, and there is not a wish or desire that the Lord has implanted in our hearts in righteousness but will be realized."[13]

One of the greatest desires of Eliza's heart was realized in October of 1872, when she traveled to the Holy Land with her brother Lorenzo and a group of Church leaders. In February, at the beginning of the year, Leonora died—the older sister who was so dear to her. So perhaps her heart was even more tender than usual, as she experienced the wonders of that sacred land, and more: the trip continued for nearly nine months, covering a distance of twenty-five thousand miles!

"By 1875 Eliza was giving counsel and direction for virtually every program in which Mormon women were engaged at the ward level: home industry, silk cultivation, obstetrical training, and grain storage."[14] She also willingly involved herself in organizing the bicentennial exhibition to be held in Philadelphia and the Territorial Fair, held in Salt Lake City.

Eliza was the standard; Eliza was the trusted spiritual guide. A description of her published in the *Juvenile Instructor* in 1888 is both powerful and tender:

> She was slightly above medium height and of a slender build; her bearing was at once graceful and dignified. Hers was a noble countenance, the forehead being unusually high and expansive and the features of a slightly Hebrew cast, exquisitely cut as those of an artistic specimen of the sculptor's art. The most striking feature of all (was) those wonderful eyes, deep, penetrating, full of meaning and intelligence, often illumined with poetic fire. They were indeed the windows of a noble soul. Her conversation was charming, every word being distinctly articulated . . . In speech and action she was thoughtful and deliberate.[15]

When John Taylor became the prophet after Brigham Young's death, he nominated Eliza R. Snow in 1880 to be president of the Relief Society of the Church of Jesus Christ in all the world. At this time Eliza was seventy-six years old.

Zion's Poetess composed more than five hundred poems—personal, doctrinal, and historical—throughout her life. Many of her poems were written to friends as expressions of tender love, support, sympathy, and testimony.

Brigham Young's death in August of 1877 must have seemed like the end of an era that had encompassed all the vital spiritual events and personal journeys of her life. She lived for ten years after Brigham, and during that time she used the name of Joseph, so that she went by Eliza R. Snow Smith. As those years progressed and she came closer to the possible time of her own death, "she requested that no black be worn at her funeral—and the Assembly Hall on Temple Square was decked in beautiful white draperies and white flowers."[16] Eliza also set into words, from the quiet depths of her own spirit, what might be called a poet's epitaph:

'Tis not the tribute of a sigh From sorrow's heaving bosom drawn,
Nor tears that flow from pity's eye, to weep for me when I am gone,
No costly balm, no rich perfume, No vain sepulchral rite I claim:
No mournful knell, no marble tomb, Nor sculptur'd stone to tell my name,
In friendship's mem'ry let me live. . . for friendship holds a secret cord,

That with the fibres of my heart, Entwines so deep, so close; 'tis hard
For death's dissecting hand to part! I feel the low responses roll,
Like the far echo of the night, And whisper softly through my soul,
I would not be forgotten quite.[17]

I have often walked to the end of the quiet, enclosed Young family
burial ground in Salt Lake City, where Eliza rests serenely, close to the
grave of Brigham. I have laid flowers there, and thought tender thoughts
of her, spirit to spirit—remembering that last line.

ENDNOTES

1. Turley, *Women of Faith*, 390–91.
2. Beecher, *Eliza R. Snow: The Personal Writings of*, 10.
3. Davidson, *Eliza*, 15.
4. Beecher, 12.
5. Ibid., 12–13.
6. Snow, *The Complete Poetry*, 183.
7. Beecher, 16.
8. *Daughters in My Kingdom*, 12.
9. Ibid., 14–15.
10. Beecher, 17.
11. Trail Diary, 115–16, February 1846 through May 1847.
12. Ibid. 126.
13. Davidson, 199.
14. Ibid., 136–37.
15. lds.org/ensign/1973/09/eliza-r-snow-first-lady-of-the
    -pioneers?lang=eng).
16. "Eliza R. Snow," *Mormon Wiki*, mormonwiki.com/Eliza_R._Snow.
17. Snow, "My Epitaph," 176.

ELIZABETH ANN
SMITH WHITNEY

ELIZABETH ANN WAS BORN THE day after Christmas—a "gift of the season" baby, who was to prove a true gift to many hundreds of women as the beauties of her life unfolded.

When Ann, as she was called, left her home in Connecticut to travel with her aunt, Sarah Smith, to Ohio, she was expecting a bit of excitement, and perhaps somewhat of a different life, for Ohio was still part of the frontier. One of the men she met was a gentle, kindly fur trader who was also an enterprising man of business. She and Newel K. Whitney were married in 1822 and settled in the small town of Kirtland, Ohio. Newel opened a store, which was in a good location, and received even greater patronage when the Erie Canal was completed.

The couple became involved with the Campbellites but were quickly disenchanted with their beliefs and prayed sincerely together for further light and knowledge. In 1829, when they were praying "to the Father to be shown the way, the Spirit rested upon us," Ann recorded, "and a cloud overshadowed the house—the house passed away from our vision . . . a solemn awe pervaded us. We saw the cloud and felt the Spirit of the Lord. Then we heard a voice out of the cloud saying, 'Prepare to receive the word of the Lord, for it is coming.'"[1]

We can imagine their astonishment, and somewhat guarded delight, when Joseph Smith, young and vital with enthusiasm, burst suddenly upon them. Joseph and Emma drove up, Joseph jumped down, went in and, in Anne's words "reached his hand across the counter to my husband, called him by name, and said, 'Newel, thou art the man!.'" Newel replied that the stranger had the advantage of him, for he could not call him by name in return.

Joseph responded, "I am Joseph the Prophet. You have prayed me here, now what do you want of me?' My husband brought them directly to our house, and we were more than glad to welcome them and share with them all the comforts and blessings we enjoyed."

"As soon as I heard the Gospel as the Elders preached it," Elizabeth later said, "I knew it to be the voice of the Good Shepherd."[2]

The Whitney store soon became the headquarters of the Church, and the School of the Prophets lectures were held there. The Kirtland Temple was built, and some of the richest blessings of the gospel were enjoyed there for the first time. "At the first patriarchal blessing meeting held in the temple, Ann received the gift of 'inspirational singing', as she called it. Joseph Smith called her 'the sweet songstress of Zion' and promised her that if she remained faithful, she would never lose the gift of singing in the pure Adamic tongue. Just a year before her death, she sang for her friends—exercising that spiritual gift for the last time."[3]

Newel and Ann took seriously their role of helping those in need. In January of 1836 they hosted at their own home a three-day feast for the poor—being very close to pure in their Christ-like example to others.

The Whitneys never actually lived in Missouri, though their goods, which they sent ahead, were destroyed and their store burned. Anne remained in Greene County, Illinois, with her children, while Newel traveled back to Kirtland to settle things there. Her oldest son was able to teach school, and they were well treated until it was learned that they were Mormons. Then persecution found them with a vengeance. Those who had at first befriended them helped them cross the river at night, with Newell fortunately able to be with them. They spent the winter in Quincy, Illinois, before going up to be with the Saints at Nauvoo.

But soon they all became extremely ill with chills and fevers—so sick that they scarcely had the strength to wait upon one another. Joseph came and took the little family to a cottage which stood in his yard, and helped to care for them there. Anne remembered Joseph's words when he and Emma were living with the Whitney's in Kirtland: "That even as we had done by him, in opening our doors to him and his family when he was without a home; even so should we in the future be received by him into his house."[4]

They later lived in the rooms above Joseph's brick store, actually during the period that the Relief Society was organized there, on March 17, 1842. Elizabeth Ann was called as a counselor to Emma Smith. Also during this period Joseph received the revelation on celestial marriage. Ann's husband, Newel, was one of the first to whom Joseph revealed this new principle. They gave their eldest daughter, as the first one to enter plural marriage. Ann had explicit faith in Joseph and in the Spirit which directed and upheld him. Her faith and obedience were remarkable.

The patient couple at last built a home on Parley Street, where there was some comfort and order. However, Ann wrote: "But still we suffered many privations, which in our own home in Ohio would probably never have fallen to our lot but we always felt we must be thus tried to prepare us for further exaltation, and that we might be able to participate with those whom God had approved and owned, who 'came up out of great tribulation.'"[5]

Ann Whitney was the second woman, after Emma, to receive the sacred temple ordinances in the upper room of Joseph Smith's store. She also gave birth to the first child "born heir to the Holy Priesthood and Everlasting Covenant."[6] She says of this youngest daughter:

> I felt she was doubly a child of promise, not only through the priesthood, but through Joseph's promise to me when I gave him my eldest daughter to wife. He prophesied to me that I should have another daughter, who would be a strength and support to me to soothe my declining years; and in this daughter have those words been verified.
>
> My health was very poor, but I remained strong in the faith of the Gospel, and full of courage to persevere in the latter-day work. My two youngest children were frail little tender blossoms and required the most constant care.[7]

How gentle Elizabeth Ann's spirit, and how determined her faith!

Following the death of Joseph and Hyrum, carrying the devastating weight of that loss, as she and Newel did, Ann yet had the care and preparation of a large family that they might somehow gather everything together that they needed and leave Nauvoo. It was her strong desire to go with the first company to set forth.

"The people were most of them poor," she observed, "and they denied themselves every comfort they possibly could to assist in finishing the Lord's house. In the latter part of the fall of 1845 we commenced work in the Temple, *and then I gave myself, my time and attention to that mission. I worked in the Temple every day without cessation until it was closed.*"[8]

The first company of pioneer Saints left Nauvoo in February of 1845, crossing the frozen Mississippi River. Elizabeth Ann Whitney and her large family were amongst the number.

We know much less about the Whitneys' crossing of the plains than we do of Eliza's. They reached Winter Quarters in February 1846, helped to organize it, and remained there before starting for the Salt Lake Valley, which they reached on September 24, 1848. Nine of Newel and Elizabeth's children crossed the plains with them; he was fifty-three and Elizabeth Ann forty-seven.

Before Newel died two years later from bilious pleurisy, he was appointed by Brigham Young as Presiding Bishop of the Church, and was also acting as bishop of the Salt Lake 18th Ward, where he helped to find homes and employment for new immigrants. Interestingly, he also assisted Brother Brigham in securing a place for the new settlement of Ogden and helping to plan it.

His death was a terrible loss for the Church. He had been stalwart, visionary, and dependable from his first introduction to the Prophet Joseph Smith. He and Ann accepted all that was taught them and contributed all that was asked of them.

We cannot fully imagine the effects of his death on Ann. From their first innocent, heart-felt pleadings to the Lord, they had stood hand in hand, their spirits intertwined harmoniously, so the loss of him was truly a loss of part of Ann's self.

Appointed matron of the Endowment House by Brigham Young, Ann served in that calling, as well as many another, until late in her life when her health no longer permitted.

Ann Whitney was very generally known amongst the Saints as "Mother Whitney" and, at times, even referred to as "The Comforter," for many received blessings of comfort and even of healing at her hand.

Eliza R. Snow and other sisters had been working tirelessly to organize the women of the Church as they had at first been organized by the Prophet Joseph in Nauvoo. When the fist general presidency of the Relief Society was at last organized, Eliza R. Snow called Ann Whitney as one of her counselors. She was eighty years old at the time but served with a willing heart for the two last years of her mortal life. Her testimony remained as strong and sparkling with life as it ever had been. In a short biography written for the *Woman's Exponent* she affirmed:

> If there are any principles which have given me strength, and by which I have learned to live more truly a life of usefulness, it seems to me I could wish to impart this joy and strength to others; to tell them what the Gospel has been and is to me, ever since I embraced it and learned to live by its laws. *A fresh revelation of the Spirit day by day; an unveiling of mysteries which before were dark, deep, unexplained and incomprehensible; a most implicit faith in a divine power, in infinite truth emanating from God the Father.*[9]

When Elizabeth Ann Whitney died on February 15, 1882, she was half a year shy of eighty-two and could claim the privilege of being the second oldest member of the Church at that time. But she had lived thirty-two long years without the husband she loved. We can see that in the lines of her face as she gazes out at the camera, dressed in a belted black dress with lace gloves enfolding her long, still feminine fingers. Her face is scarcely lined with age, but there is a gentleness about it, and her deep eyes reflect years of patience; hers is the all-accepting gaze of faith.

Let us end with that last historic time when Elizabeth Ann sang, in her still-sweet voice, for the sisters who loved her. We can quite easily picture the women gathered in quiet anticipation to hear their beloved sister sing. Too few times have they heard her, and this may be the last. The strains of her lovely voice stream into the stillness of the room, and settle in the corners, trembling in the minds of the listeners with the benediction of a history, both tragic and blessed, that is uniquely their own.

Her words, in the Adamic tongue—are they known to many? It does not really matter. The words are there, and their meaning, and their memories—and the beauty of a face, sanctified by both desires and deeds, that mark her as one of the noble daughters of her heavenly Father and Mother.

ENDNOTES

1. *Daughters in My Kingdom*, 128.
2. Ibid.
3. Madsen, *In Their Own Words*, 196.
4. Whitney, *Reminiscences*, 200.
5. Ibid., 203.
6. Whitney, "A Leaf from an Autobiography," *Woman's Exponent*, August 1, 1873, 33, as quoted in *Daughters in My Kingdom,* 129.
7. Whitney, *Reminiscences*, 204.
8. Ibid., 205.
9. Whitney, "A Leaf from an Autobiography," 33.

FAR WEST, MISSOURI

Very early in the development of the Church, many members moved to Jackson County, Missouri. But the old citizens found much to criticize and condemn. At length, in 1833, twelve hundred Saints were driven from Far West and other settlements, until at last the Missouri legislature created Caldwell County, in a far corner of Missouri which no one wanted, where only a few bee-keeping settlers lived.

This was in 1836. In 1838 the Lord revealed to Joseph that Far West would be "a holy and consecrated land"[1] and that they were to again build a temple to his name. But their enemies, gathered into mobs, would not leave them alone. Nearly eight hundred men, under a Presbyterian preacher named Woods, prepared to attack DeWitt, and would have destroyed it if Generals Doniphan and Parks had not stopped them.

So it came to pass in Far West as well, culminating in Governor Boggs' order to the state militia to surround Far West, followed, at the end of October, with Boggs' infamous Extermination Order, stating that "the Mormons must be treated as enemies and must be exterminated or driven from the state."[2]

Joseph, Hyrum, and other leaders of the Church were imprisoned, and the atrocities of Far West increased, until Brigham and the remaining Twelve signed a covenant that they would not leave any of the poor and needy in the state.

This was a time of incomprehensible suffering, but also an outpouring of miracles experienced by many of the Saints.

ENDNOTES

1. "Far West," *Church History Topics*, churchofjesuschrist.org/study /history/topics/far-west?lang=eng.
2. McCloud, *Joseph Smith: A Photobiography*, 85.

LEONORA
CANNON TAYLOR

LEONORA'S LIFE, FROM START TO finish, rings true to the statement the English poet, Lord Byron, made: "For truth is oft'times strange; stranger than fiction."[1]

Leonora was raised on the Isle of Man, in the seaside village of Peel. The isle sits alone in the Irish Sea, off the northwest corner of England, and is a mere thirty miles long and ten miles wide. Her island was a lovely, almost mythical place, with grey seals, minke whales, and sometimes sharks that basked along the shores.

Peel was a fishing port, busy with seamen and merchants, and narrow winding streets and lanes that led down to the quayside. Leonora's father was a successful sea captain, and his family enjoyed many of the comforts and advantages of this prosperity.

Her father, George, had married his sweetheart, Leonora Callister, and there was a family of nine children when he died suddenly during a mutiny at sea. From that moment on, Leonora's life would be fraught with a variety of challenges.

She was the eldest, and now had to do her part in supporting the family. She found a position as a lady's companion, but this required her to live in London, a place very different from her home by the sea.

For a time she was able to return to the island and actually live in the ancient castle Rushen in Castletown. Here she was in the company of many distinguished people, one of whom, a Mr. Mason, entreated her to come with his daughter to Canada, where he had been appointed private secretary to the new governor-general of that land. The two girls were already fast friends, but Leonora knew she would be walking away from her family forever if she were to leave.

As she struggled to decide, Leonora had a dream which she interpreted as directing her to go.

Once in Toronto she found and joined a Methodist study group, for she had associated with this sect in London. The class was led by a young Englishman by the name of John Taylor. And why did he happen to get moony-eyed over her? He was handsome, yes, but only twenty-four years old, and very unpolished and unlearned in his ways. She rejected his importuning, saying no nearly a dozen times. One reason for this was the fact that John Taylor was twenty-four years old—and Leonora was thirty-six!

But again a dream came to direct her, and she accepted John's offer and married him on January 28, 1833.

They remained devout Methodists. He continued at his work as a turner, and four children were born to them by the spring of 1836 when Parley P. Pratt, an apostle, knocked on their door. He, too, had followed promptings of the Spirit, despite debts he was desirous of paying and a wife who was ill. But Heber C. Kimball had pronounced a prophecy and blessing upon his head, so he traveled in faith to Canada and, with a letter of introduction, went to the Taylor home.

John was annoyed that his friend had written an introduction for a Mormon! He treated the man with courtesy, but nothing more. Parley had been promised that he would find "a people prepared for the fullness of the Gospel."[2] He tried several congregations in the city, but no one wanted to hear what he had to say.

He returned that first evening to the Taylor home, rather despondent in spirit. But Leonora had been thinking, and told her neighbor who had come to visit, Mrs. Walton, that she would be sad to see this man leave, for "he may be a man of God."

"Well, now I understand the feelings and spirit which brought me to your house at this time," Mrs. Walton responded. She sought out Parley Pratt and offered her home for his study groups, and offered help in finding a congregation where he might preach."[3]

John and Leonora *were* open to the truth; everything in their hearts responded. They were baptized May 9, 1836. They took their two young children, left their home, and journeyed to Kirtland, Ohio, where the members of the Church had gathered. Leonora thought she would find a warm, welcoming community of Latter-day Saints, and was shocked and saddened to experience instead cruelty and harsh intolerance.

They moved on quickly to Missouri, arriving in the fall of 1838, just as the infamous Extermination Order of Governor Boggs, issued on October 27, was being put into effect. The mobs became bold and ferocious, spoiling Far West: the farms, the houses; even killing the cattle and forbidding the hungry Saints to use their own animals for food.

Their escape from the horrors of Missouri led them to the Iowa side of the Mississippi; the village of Montrose, standing across the river from Nauvoo. John was with his little family for only a snatch of time, being one of the apostles called to serve a mission to England. Leonora was sick with a fever, and all of her children were intermittently gravely ill with chills and fevers.

What could wife and husband do? John Taylor blessed his wife and little children, and dedicated them into the care of the Lord, that His loving arms might enclose, protect and comfort them. George, the eldest of their three children, was but six years old. Wife and children were living in a room in one of the old barracks, twenty feet square, with one small window in the back door, which was "of the hinges and walls so open that a skunk came in every Night one Winter."

The children did not understand. She tells her husband: "Poor Mary Ann often crys for you. If she sees me look sorrowful she begins to cry that moment for you and I can scarce stop her."[4]

Leonora later confessed, "I had gone through everything but death during his absence."[5]

In one letter, penned September 9, 1839, Leonora wrote: "Pray write soon and often to me My Dear John. I never needed more grace, patience or your prayers than I do at present."[6]

From time to time she literally despaired of her children's lives, one right after another, so it seemed. She was so ill she had to wean her baby, who then became seriously ill, cried all the first night, so that her heart felt near to broken. In a letter to her husband, who must have seemed lost to her in the midst of a land and a place far and unknown, she wrote: "All this time George was my only help. He went to the well and did all he could—(remember that George is only a lad of six). On Sunday he fell back to the floor in a Fit and had Chile and Feaver. I watched him all night. Today he came to himself so as to talk to me." but George did not *stay* well, and Leonora relates struggle after struggle trying to keep her children alive. She adds, "My dear John I hope the Lord will not lay more upon me than I am able to bear."[7]

An unexpected blessing came from John Taylor's mission to the homeland. Leonora's brother, George Cannon, was converted to the gospel, along with his wife, Ann Quayle. This was a delight to Leonora, who loved her brother dearly, and the Cannons were powerful converts who soon became leaders in the kingdom, and in moving the work along.

But day to day living was still a very challenging thing. Leonora became involved as one of the eighteen charter members of the Nauvoo Relief Society and in works of mercy to those more needy than she. She saw her husband grow, and the two of them grew closer together, and more and more devoted to the work.

John had returned to Nauvoo in 1841, and became immediately active as judge advocate of the Legion, a regent of the University of Nauvoo, member of the city council, and, at the same time, somehow managed to build a lovely, stately home for his family. We cannot imagine what this must have meant to Leonora, who had still been living in the old barracks upon his return!

In 1842 their second daughter died fifteen months after her birth. Leonora's sister-in-law Ann Cannon had died at sea, and her brother, George, going to St. Louis, Missouri, after his arrival in Nauvoo, died after only six months at that place. John and Leonora took their niece, Ann, and young nephew, George Q., into their home and raised them as their own.

During this same period of time, the principle of plural wives was introduced. John, in horror, fought and refused it as long as he could. He and Leonora faced the challenge together, but it was always very difficult for her.

Time was running out, though none of the Saints really knew it as yet. Late in June John Taylor accompanied Joseph and Hyrum Smith to the nearby city of Carthage, where the brothers were consigned, without trial, into the local jail. Several of the brethren accompanied them, but after two days they were sent out one by one, on various errands, and denied re-admittance, until at last only two of the apostles, John Taylor and Willard Richards, remained.

These four, left together, knew what was to happen. But they knew also in whose hands they were. Late in the afternoon of June 27, John sang, in his clear baritone voice, all the verses to the song "A Poor Wayfaring Man of Grief," melancholy with its message of suffering, sacrifice, and love. Joseph was deeply moved and asked his friend to sing it again.

About five in the afternoon the jailer entered, intending to move the men back to a more removed, safer cell. But there was suddenly a loud commotion of voices and shots, and the narrow stairs were swept with a dozen loud, awkward feet, with the oaths and the gunshots, and the thick gray of gunpowder—and the four innocent men, stunned, attempting to find some means to defend themselves.

Hyrum was the first to die, facing the direct shot through the unlocked door which the mobbers were attempting to break down. John ran for the small window and tried to jump, but a ball crashed into his left thigh, tearing it to the bone. Precariously he teetered there until another struck the watch in his pocket, which threw him back into the room. All together, four balls entered his body. At the same time the Prophet attempted to jump from the window, was struck, and fell, crying, "O Lord, my God!"

Willard Richards, a large man, was miraculously unhurt, in fulfillment of Joseph's prophecy concerning him, and it was he who at first hid John Taylor, hoping to thus save his life, and later cared for him at the Hamilton House and saw that his wounds were dressed. The next day the two men returned to Nauvoo with the bodies of the Prophet and patriarch—and Leonora for the first time was able to learn what had befallen her husband!

She had most probably heard the night before of the murder of Joseph and Hyrum. But what of Wilford Woodruff and John Taylor? As she prayed in the silent hours for the safety of her husband, did an assurance come to her that he was alive, that he would be returned to her?

She received word the following morning that John Taylor had been wounded but was all right. When the wagon rolled into Nauvoo and she saw the extent of the damages that her husband had suffered (though he did his best to soften this for her), what were the reactions that shook her heart and mind?

Of course, we cannot ever know, nor hardly even imagine what her experience was like. But all that she had become through the intense trials of her life—through the patient faith, through the selfless, obedient choices she had made—all this must have come to her aid at this terrible hour. But in the midst of caring for her suffering husband, she turned all her pluck, energy, and even anguish into a letter of appeal which she wrote to Illinois Governor Ford, pleading for the safety of Nauvoo, and entreating that the murderers of the Prophet be brought to justice. No reply was ever afforded her.

The Taylors left the beloved City of Joseph along with the other Saints, but soon after their arrival in Winter Quarters John was called on a mission to England. The wives struggled to establish themselves, wait in patience, and pray for their husband's health and well-being. Leonora was separated from John roughly half of their marriage, giving him over to the work of the Lord.

When he returned he brought treasures, including instruments which Orson Pratt would use in the future to lay out the city of Salt Lake. They left Winter Quarters and arrived in the Valley in early October 1847.

Leonora leaves a few lovely "wisps" of ideas and impressions of the unusual journey. On September 2 she recorded, "Found many beautiful stones"—indicating her love of beauty, and a bit of a child's enthusiasm for simple things. She also recorded on Tuesday the 7th: "Meeting with the sisters. Dinner for Pioneers and volunteers, about a hundred sat down, they had a dance after, the 12 met in Council, unil 11 o'clock. It snowed until the afternoon when it became fine, the 12 breakfasted with us and started for Winter Quarters. Picked currants.

"Sunday: started late. An ox was missing. I went up and down a steep hill. Rob Gardner's child ran over. Traveled 13 m."

Early in August she records that they were visited by two hundred Sioux Indians, and their associations with the Indians all seemed remarkably friendly. On October 6 Leonora writes simply, "Entered valley of Salt Lake." She also recorded in this place: "I feel and know in all my trials that the Lord is near and that He blesses and comforts my heart, and they that trust in the Lord shall never fear."[8]

John was in the midst of all the growth and excitement of the desert kingdom. Leonora participated, especially in support of the growing women's efforts and organizations. But her heart was also content to, in some ways, sit back and enjoy her family—and perhaps ponder the memories of the strange and remarkable things that had happened to her since she left the island and the sea of her childhood, and since that day, in another place far distant from this desert inland, when she listened to Parley P. Pratt, the Mormon missionary, and, sad at his impending departure, told her neighbor, "He may be a man of God."

Leonora died on December 9, 1868, at the age of seventy-two. She did not live to see her husband become the prophet and third president of the Church. But Leonora was still a very vital part of what he was.

Among the notes she recorded on the back page of her diary was this: "The Lord often led me by a way that I knew not and in a path that I naturally did not wish to go, every sweet had its bitter, the way seemed to me narrower every day. Without his almighty power to me, I cannot walk in it. To whom shall I go or look for succor but unto thee my Father and only Friend."[9]

ENDNOTES

1. Quotable Quote, goodreads.com/quotes/360520-for-truth-is-always-strange-stranger-than-fiction.
2. *Autobiography of Parlye Parker Pratt (1807–1857)*, boap.org/LDS/Early-Saints/PPPratt.html.
3. Jensen, "John Taylor Family," 52; see also *Parley P. Pratt Autobiography*, 130–36.
4. Ibid., 416.
5. Madsen, *In Their Own Words*, 191.
6. Turley, *Women of Faith*, 414.
7. Ibid. 417.
8. Ibid., 419.
9. Roberts, *Life of John Taylor*, 474, as quoted in *Women of Faith*, 419.

BATHSHEBA BIGLER SMITH

BATHSHEBA BIGLER WAS BORN MAY 3, 1822, and raised in the beauty, comfort, and ease of an upper class Southern household. Her father had a three-hundred-acre plantation in Shinnston, Virginia. Although she was the eighth of nine children, she enjoyed all the advantages of plantation life, and the training which made a gentlewoman of her: hospitality, management, and handwork, which included spinning, weaving, and embroidery.

She was fifteen when her family joined the Church, and her life was forever changed. Writing of her early testimony, Bathsheba said: "I believed the Book of Mormon to be a divine record, and that Joseph Smith was a Prophet of God. I knew by the spirit of the Lord, which I received in answer to prayer, that these things were true. On the 21st of August 1837, I was baptized."[1]

One of the missionaries who brought the gospel to them was George A. Smith, a cousin of the Prophet Joseph. At once they both felt a deep attraction and, though she was a sophisticated Southern belle, that did not stand in the way of the pledge they made to one another that "with the blessings of the Almighty in preserving us, in three years' time from this time, we will be married."[2]

In the fall of 1837 her family traveled to join with the Saints in Far West, Missouri. Bathsheba records that the young people enjoyed the journey and thought it romantic to travel over beautiful country, with no chores or other work to do.

But their rude awakening came when they entered the state and found bands of angry men surrounding their wagon, with cruel words and threats. However, their unusual response was, "As you are Virginians, we will let you go on, but we believe you will soon return, for you will quickly become convinced of your folly."[3]

Leaving the nightmares of Far West as soon as possible, they traveled with the thousands of other displaced Saints, heading for the Mississippi River and the state of Illinois beyond. Bathsheba, with a cheerful consideration, gave up her seat on the wagon to the sick and ailing, and walked most of the way.

As with many of the other Saints, the Biglers stayed first in Quincy, just across the river. Both Bathsheba and her father were struck with the dreaded malaria, from which she was able to recover. But her father died, and they were forced to go on without him into this unknown life which awaited them.

How many families—destitute, desolate really—shared much the same fate? What quietly grand and noble spirits these were, who continued to go on, in faith.

George A., much of this time, had been serving a mission to England. After his return, the two, sure still of their choice, were married, on July 25, 1841. Bathsheba was eager to set up housekeeping on her own—but not five different times in a year! Her new dwellings were shabby and inadequate, small and cold, with leaking roofs or smoking chimneys. Bathsheba, at nineteen, was the youngest member of the new Relief Society. But she was self-reliant, and she did not mind hard work.

In 1842 George built a lovely two-story home for Bathsheba, which promised to be comfortable and dry. She was expecting their first child, so they hurried to complete the house, moving in just twelve days before George Jr. was born.

Their idyllic days were short; within two months George was called on a mission to the eastern states. He went with her blessing, and in his absence she busied herself with her garden and with the care of her home. She prided herself on her self-reliance and efficiency. She also loved to serve and, as Relief Society grew too large to fit into the small upper room above Joseph Smith's store, she joined cheerfully with the others to meet outside, until the weather should prevent them.

She kept her own sorrows and heartaches to herself, save what she revealed in the letters she sent to her beloved husband. In one she wrote: "I look at your portrait which I never forget. It hangs back of my bed and is the last thing I see and the first in the morning. Oh, it is such a comfort to me. It always looks pleasant and kind, as you do, and seems to say when I feel bad, 'Cheer up, all is well' . . . When the shades of night fall upon it, it does look so much like you that it makes the tears fall fast."[4]

The events in Nauvoo were unsettling, as Joseph Smith's enemies, and the enemies of the Church, moved in. Joseph had to defend himself against all kinds of calumny, especially the accusation that he had attempted to kill Governor Boggs of Missouri—the same man who had issued the Extermination Order against the Saints. But there was a period of peace from January to June of 1843, in which Joseph was able to instruct and reveal to his brethren all that was necessary for the pure gospel of Jesus Christ to go forward after his death.

After submitting to the enraged mobs who desired his life, both Joseph and Hyrum were shot to death in Carthage jail. Among all the other sensations she felt, Bathsheba must have remembered her initial assessment of the Prophet when she first saw him: "He was splendid looking, a large man, tall and fair. He had a very nice complexion. His eyes were blue, and his hair a golden brown and very pretty. My first impressions were that he was an extraordinary man. He was different from any other man I ever saw; had the most heavenly countenance; was genial, affable and kind; and looked the soul of honor and integrity."[5]

A month and a half after the Martyrdom, George and Bathsheba's daughter was born, and named Bathsheba after her mother.

As the Saints prepared to leave their beloved home, now called the City of Joseph, they turned nearly every house into a wagon shop or, in Bathsheba's case, a paint shop, which she accepted with her usual cheerful air. From December 1845 to February 1846, she also worked in the finally completed Nauvoo Temple, giving thousands of endowments to the anxious Saints. On January 25, 1846, she, George, and their two children were sealed together, for eternity as well as time.

Bathsheba, along with others of the women, left her little house swept and clean, "then with emotions in my heart I gently closed the door and faced an unknown future, faced it with faith in God and with no less assurance of the ultimate establishment of the Gospel in the West and of the enduring principles, than I had felt in those trying scenes in Missouri."[6]

Bathsheba's faith also saw her through the introduction of polygamy and her offering of four worthy and virtuous women to be George's wives.

She had no time to fuss about such matters; she left them all in the hands of the Lord. She knew how deeply George A. loved her; she often boasted that they were "lovers all their lives."

When they left Nauvoo and crossed the Mississippi, the weather was so bitter cold that the river froze over, and consequently hundreds of families could drive their heavy wagons safely over the ice.

She describes vividly the challenges of establishing a settlement where the Saints could tarry until they were able to travel West: "I will not try to describe how we traveled through storms of snow wind and rain, how roads had to be made, bridges built, and rafts constructed; how our poor animals had to drag on day after day with scanty food; how our camps suffered from poverty, sickness and death . . . the Lord was with us, and his power was made manifest daily in our journey."[7]

March in Winter Quarters was not pleasant, nor easy. Bathsheba does not record whether George was with her or away when her mother died, on the eleventh of the month. Now she was an orphan, with no ties to the beauty and security of her life as a child. Three weeks after her mother's death, Bathsheba gave birth to a son. They gave the little one the name of John, but he lived only four hours. He was with her mother now, but Bathsheba had scarcely held him in her arms, and she was bereft.

In the summer of 1847 many of the Saints were prepared, and pulled out of Winter Quarters. Bathsheba had agreed to stay, to wait—was not waiting a constant portion of a woman's life then?—to stay while George took several trips back and forth from the Salt Lake Valley, helping others to make the journey to the Valley.

Two years; two years is a very long time. Many Saints came and went while Bathsheba set her own longings and curiosity aside. When it was at last her turn, she was prepared to make much of it: George had both widened and heightened her wagon; she carpeted the floor, placed four chairs in the center, hung a candlestick, looking glass, and pincushion where they would ride safely. She also made room to carry her paintings of George A., her parents, and Joseph and Hyrum Smith. Bathsheba had actually received formal lessons in portraiture from William W. Major, who was a British convert to the Church.

The journey was long and somewhat hazardous, but Bathsheba kept her sense of humor, even when her wagon was nearly swept downstream, through a cattle stampede, and a thirty-six hour snowstorm.

Their first home in the Valley was close to the house of Bathsheba's sister, Melissa, which helped, since George was often away with Church responsibilities. Truth is surely stranger than fiction, for her sister's little daughter Julina spent countless happy hours at Bathsheba's, playing with her daughter, little Bathsheba. Perhaps her sister had challenges that contributed to the arrangement, for by the time she was seven, Julina lived with her aunt, though she went every day to visit her mother.

When George was called as Church historian in 1854, the family "moved in," living in one half of the building, with the other half being offices. Their home, wherever it was, became a natural center for get-togethers, simple entertainments of singing, reading, playing musical instruments, and even dancing. George Jr. played the flute and the fife—and both he and his sister played the drums! "They made our homes joyous with song," Bathsheba wrote, "and just their pleasure was mine; I was so proud of them and so happy to be with them."[8]

A few years later, George Jr. went on a mission to Southern Utah to teach the Moquis Indians. He was but eighteen years old, yet held the office of Seventy. He was with Jacob Hamblin's group of eight or nine other men when he became separated from his comrades, going after his horse which had run off. The Navajo were angry because a group of US troops had attacked their settlement, killing the old men, women, and children. George A. was easy game, and his young life was forfeited.

His cruel loss was nearly more than Bathsheba could bear. Two months later her daughter, Bathsheba, married, and it was good that young Julina still lived with her.

Bathsheba had always wanted a large posterity, and so she was granted: fourteen children from her daughter and ten from Julina. These children were a source of great comfort and joy to her.

She was also able to travel with her beloved George, visiting wards and branches of the Church. They were always warmly received. Bathsheba was happy. She knew how precious and rare her marriage was.

When George A. died in September of 1875 Bathsheba wrote: "His head lay . . . against my bosom, good angels had come to receive his precious spirit . . . but he was gone, my light, my sun, my life, my joy."[9]

Twelve years later she was called away from her beloved grandchildren to serve as counselor to Zina Young in the General Relief Society presidency. The two old friends accomplished much during the thirteen years they served together, including support of the establishment of an

LDS hospital in 1884. Zina died in 1901 and Bathsheba was called to succeed her as president. She would be the last general Relief Society president who was also a member of the Nauvoo Relief Society.

Bathsheba continued active, facing a future of continual change: she organized training for nurses and free services for the poor, sent representatives to national and international women's meetings, and encouraged home industry, as well as contributions to help fund the construction of a women's building. The ward Relief Societies had buildings, and the brethren had buildings, but the general Relief Society had been squeezed in wherever they might fit.

This noble enterprise did not meet with success at that time, however. Not until 1956 was the Relief Society building constructed.

Bathsheba also donated Relief Society wheat wherever there was a need: the San Francisco earthquake in 1909, famine victims in China, Native Americans in need in her own state.

She also served as a temple matron during this time. In fact, Bathsheba officiated in all of the temples which were constructed during her lifetime: Nauvoo, Logan, Manti, St. George, and Salt Lake. She also lovingly administered blessings to the sick and washed and anointed sisters in confinement, prior to childbirth.[10]

Brigham Young called Bathsheba the "high priestess of righteousness, arrayed in her simple white gown of homemade silk."[11] This gown was spun and made by Bathsheba herself in the temple!

Quoting from an address in the *Woman's Exponent*, January 1906, as part of Bathsheba's testimony then, and now:

> The Prophet I recall and his wondrous spiritual power . . . rising from our weakness, in obedience to the servants of the Most High, we proceed, crossing trackless plains, fording swollen streams, scaling rugged mountain heights, and descending into 'The Valley', to find rest from persecution and comfort in the desert.
>
> All the events of those trying years unite today, revealing to me, in the evening of life, the overshadowing importance of the plan of salvation.
>
> The Spirit of God which is the Holy Ghost and the Comforter, surrounds us and pervades the Universe, and is the medium by which we may receive the inspiration of God toward intelligence and through which it is our right to receive comfort; and finally that faith, hope, and charity are necessary for divine grace, but that the greatest of these is charity.[12]

ENDNOTES

1. "Autobiography of Bathsheba W. Smith," boap.org/LDS/Early-Saints/ BWSmith.html.
2. Ibid.
3. Ibid.
4. Ibid.
5. McCloud, *Photobiography*, 1–2.
6. "Autobiography of Bathsheba W. Smith,"
7. *Daughters in My Kingdom*, 33.
8. LaRene Porter Gaunt, "Bathsheba W. Smith*," Ensign*, July 2005, churchofjesuschrist.org/study/ensign/2005/07/bathsheba-w-smith -witness-to-history?lang=eng.
9. Ibid.
10. "Bathsheba Bigler Smith," *Encyclopedia of Mormonism*, 1.
11. Bathsheba Bigler Smith, *Relief Society Women*, reliefsocietywomen .com/blog/2009/10/01/.
12. Bathsheba W. Smith, "We Have Still a Greater Mission," churchofjesuschrist.org/study/church-historians-press/at-the-pulpi /part-2/chapter-24?lang=eng.

EMMELINE B. WELLS

EMMELINE'S LIFE IS SO EXHAUSTIVE and complex that we hope to at least touch well upon the trials, challenges, and soaring accomplishments of this tender and determined little soul.

She started the adventures of her life when she was but a girl of fourteen, the youngest of seven children, living with her family in Petersham, Massachusetts, where she had been born on February 29, 1828. The first maturing influence of her early life was the death of her father, David Woodward, when she was but four years old.

Emmeline loved to learn, would always love to learn, and had a remarkably intelligent mind and a flowering interest in writing. Her mother, seeing her abilities, sent her to New Salem Academy, and while she was away, Mormon missionaries converted her mother and sister. At the age of fourteen Emmeline graduated, came home and was baptized, and taught school for a season, as young educated girls at that time often did. But her sensitive spirit suffered from the cruel criticism of many of her lifelong friends, who turned against her and reviled her for the decision she had made to be baptized.

Emmeline married James Harvey Harris, son of the branch president in New Salem, the following year, July 29, 1843, when he was sixteen, and Emmeline but fifteen! Less than a year later, in the spring of 1844, the young couple traveled with his parents and other area converts to Nauvoo. She leaves a powerful impression of her meeting with the Prophet Joseph:

> His majestic bearing, so entirely different from anyone I had ever seen, was more than a surprise . . . before I was aware of it he came to me, and when he took my hand, I was simply electrified—thrilled through and through to the tips of my fingers, and every part of my

body, as if some magic elixir had given me new life and vitality . . . the one thought that filled my soul was, 'I have seen the Prophet of God. He has taken me by the hand'. This testimony has never left me in all the "perils by the way". . . . He possessed, too, the innate refinement that one finds in the born poet, or in the most cultivated and intellectual and poetical nature . . . he was beyond my comprehension. . . . For many years, I felt it too sacred an experience even to mention.[1]

This was in the spring. On June 27, 1844, this remarkable prophet and his gentle brother, Hyrum, were murdered in Carthage Jail and, amidst the fear, confusion, and apostasy, James' parents left the Church and returned back east. In much the same moment of time, Emmeline gave birth to her first child, who was to be her only son. They named him Eugene Henri, but the delight she took in him was short-lived, for his life on earth was but six brief weeks. Burying a baby when you are yourself no more than a girl is something that many of us cannot even imagine.

Lost and alone, with no means of support for the two of them, James went up the Mississippi in search of work. So, here was Emmeline, a girl of sixteen, having gone through more than some women do in the course of their lives.

And she felt it deeply, for such was her nature. In her diary of February 20, 1845, nine days before her seventeenth birthday, she wrote: "When will sorrow leave my bosom! All my days have I experienced it, oppression has been my lot . . . is not my life a romance, indeed it is a novel strange and marvelous. Here am I brought to this great city by one to whom I ever expected to look for protection and left dependent on the mercy and friendship of strangers. . . must I forever be unhappy, wilt the time never come when happiness and enjoyment will be the lot of this lump of clay?"[2]

She records that she waited, met each boat she could, and watched them pull into Nauvoo, listening for the familiar sound of Eugene's voice, or his step. She had no word from him, and he never returned. She did not find out until much later that he had deserted the responsibilities that pressed upon him, had taken work aboard ship, and died as a sailor in the Indian Ocean.[3]

Emmeline fell back on teaching to support herself, and by the following spring she had married Newel K. Whitney as his second and only other wife. She was warmly welcomed by both Newel and his wife, Elizabeth Ann. She needed the tenderness of both of them, and responded to it with all her heart. Her new husband was thirty-three years older than she, and often she looked upon him as a father and protector.

The Whitney family left Nauvoo in February of 1846. Emmeline's mother, who had been such a faithful Latter-day Saint, died in Winter Quarters. It was easier for Emmeline to go on than to look back.

In one journal account she writes: "Mrs. Whitney, Sarah Ann, and myself crossed the river to go to the encampment of the Saints. We crossed the river a part of the way on foot, and then went on to the encampment about 1 mile beyond. . . . We repaired immediately to Mr. H. C. Kimball's tent, took supper, and slept for the first time on the ground. There was a snowstorm without, yet all was peace and harmony within."[4]

Emmeline wrote detailed, picturesque descriptions. After first joining and seeing for herself the pioneer camp, she wrote: "It looked like pictures I have seen of the ancients pitching their tents and journeying from place to place with their cattle and their goods."[5]

Again she drew a word picture for us: "Just across the creek someone had set the prairie on fire. How we were to cross, this was a question. It ran like lightning through the grass making a crackling among the bushes resembling the noise of burning crackers."[6]

Emmeline endured not only the hardships of the journey but a pregnancy, which resulted in a daughter, born in the wagon that carried them forth. During the journey Brother Whitney often prophesied of Emmeline's future and the work she would be able to do. The fulfillment of his words seemed impossible to her young mind. Nevertheless, she loved and trusted him entirely, and so cherished in her heart the things he had told her.

They reached the Valley on October 8, 1848, and Emmeline was pregnant with a second child. A family home was constructed, and she had her second daughter there. Melvina was born on August 18, and there seemed much reason for Emmeline to rejoice. But six weeks later, the gentle Newel Whitney died suddenly, leaving a bereaved and stunned family. Emmeline was a widow twice by the time she was twenty-two. Now, with a new infant and a small daughter to support, she turned again to teaching, trying to put together the fragmented pieces of her life.

Teaching was challenging and uncertain, with many students who only paid in kind. At last, tired and discouraged, Emmeline wrote a letter to Daniel H. Wells, one of Newel's best friends, asking him to "consider the lonely state of his friend's widow" and accept her as a wife.[7]

This may appear strange, yet it was not so for the times. Daniel Wells was already a polygamist, with five wives, though his first wife left and divorced him when he traveled West with the Saints. He had a large family home, but it was already filled to the gills. He gave Emmeline a lovely little house of her own. But she was lonely, as this busy man was mayor of Salt Lake, head of public works for the Church, and half a dozen other things, and his path did not lead past the place where she lived. She would sometimes go weeks without even seeing him, save at public events.

Three more daughters were born to her and this half-husband, half-stranger. She named the second Elizabeth Ann Whitney Wells, after Newel's wife, whom she admired and loved, and the third was Louisa.

She raised her daughters, and planted a garden and a little orchard, which she lovingly tended. When Johnson's army came and the Saints had to flee their homes and move hastily across the Point of the Mountain to Provo, Emmeline made the move with the rest, and even taught school in Provo for a spell. She felt that for many intents and purposes she was still alone. She had spells of ill health and depression, but she was still able to write in her journal that she knew the Lord was mindful of her and would take care of her, as Newel had said.

In 1873 Emmeline began sending articles to the newly established *Woman's Exponent*. She was hesitant, at first using the pseudonym of Blanche Beechwood. In growing confidence she began to write under her own name, and soon secured the position of assistant editor. By 1877 she became editor, and as a stronger and stronger advocate of women's rights, she began to become nationally known.

The complications and responsibilities of Emmeline's life increased, but so did her challenges and trials. Her daughter Emma died at the young age of twenty-five. She also lost Louisa, her youngest, whom she felt the Lord would not take from her, but Louisa died in childbirth in San Francisco, leaving a stillborn son. Also during this period, in February 1882, Elizabeth Ann Whitney died. Ann had been Emmeline's sister-wife for a brief time, but also a mother-figure, and the most tender and devoted of friends.

The one earthly thing she could call her own was the small house which she had loved and cared for, planting a garden and even a small orchard. It brought her such joy and a needed sense of security. But Daniel Wells suffered a period of financial distress, and Emmeline records in 1878 the need of practicing more rigid economy.

Then, in 1887, returning from the devastation of Louisa's death, she learned that Daniel had sold her beloved house. While he managed to find small cottages for the other wives who had lost their large home as well, Emmeline somehow ended up in the old adobe Church historian's office.

Confiding her feelings to her diary helped her maintain her faith and her sense of connectedness with the Lord. She was also able to pour out the expressions of her soul in poetry, and her book of poems entitled *Musings and Memories* was not only published but also went into a second edition in 1912. At about this same time Emmeline was selected for the honor of unveiling the Seagull Monument on Temple Square at its dedication—on the celebration of her eighty-fourth birthday.

Emmeline's progress seemed to expand at a quick rate. She worked with Relief Society and Primary leaders, traveling all over Utah territory, teaching and encouraging the women and trying to meet their needs. She was involved in the National and International Councils of Women, met with six different presidents of the United States, traveled to London as well as this nation's capital, and became a close and respected lifelong friend of Susan B. Anthony. In her diary she wrote, "I desire to do all in my power to help elevate the conditions of my own people, women especially."[8]

She did this in remarkable ways, for she brought respect and then honor for Utah and Mormon women through her suffrage activities, and through the example of bold, yet gentle Mormon womanhood. She did not shirk from defending polygamy, strongly ascertaining the many advantages of plural marriage "as a form of liberation, for when wives lived in the same home, each woman was free to pursue individual interests because child care and housework were shared. Most also enjoyed the companionship of their sister wives."[9]

She never became too busy or too important to serve wherever she was needed. In 1876 Brigham Young asked her to direct a project that required the sisters of the Church to gather and store large quantities of wheat. Through the offices of Relief Society she pleaded for support, asking the women to glean and gather even what wheat they found along fence lines, and in ditch banks, trusting the Prophet to know what use this gathered wheat would serve, some of the amazing 10,000 bushes used, as ever, to succor the poor. But the Relief Society was able to sell more than 200,000 bushes to the United States during World War I and, after the war, President Woodrow Wilson and his wife paid Emmeline a personal visit in her home, expressing their appreciation for the vital, life-saving work she had done.

Emmeline was forty-nine years old in 1877 when she became editor of the *Woman's Exponent,* and for the next thirty-seven years it was the passion of her life. Published twice monthly, it became a lifeline for LDS women everywhere.

For twenty-two years Emmeline served as secretary to several presidents of the general Relief Society. For nearly thirty years she represented Utah in the fight for statehood and women's rights—at the same time running the *Woman's Exponent* and maintaining a close relationship with her five daughters.

Her energy seemed boundless, and the driving force of her will was recognized by all. She could be caustic at times, and critical, but the effusion of her heart was poured out in the love she bestowed on all, and her human failings were small and inconsequential in comparison.

She fought her inner devils, her insecurities, her unmet longings and needs. Yet, Emmeline was greatly loved by leaders in the women's movement. Years after the International Council of Women's meeting in London in 1899, at which Emmeline spoke, the countess of Aberdeen, who was president of the council, spent a day in Utah, enjoying the association with old friends there. At the end of her visit she made an interesting statement, expressing her pleasure at "the honor of being introduced twice in one day by a queen, for in my brief visit here I have quickly observed that 'Aunt Em' is the Queen of Utah."[10]

She was often affectionately called "Aunt Em." And the warmth of her spirit expanded with unanticipated joy when her husband, Daniel H. Wells, was appointed president of the Manti Temple and began urging her to accompany him there. She was sixty-two and Daniel seventy-six. But she records: "O the joy of being once more in his dear presence . . . we are more like lovers than husband and wife, for we have been so far removed from each other . . . how odd it seems. I do not feel old, neither does he—we are young to each other and that is well."[11]

The following summer and fall were rich with time spent together, but in March 1891, Daniel Wells lay dying, and Emmeline reached his bed in Salt Lake City in time to spend the last few days with him before he died.

She was grateful for the intense joy of her relationship with him. As her poem "Faith and Fidelity" expressed it:

And so some lives go on in tragedies, each part
To be sustained by human effort grand;
Though 'neath the outward seeming lies the broken heart,
That only One above can understand.[12]

In 1910 Emmeline was called as the fifth general president of the Relief Society. She served until 1921, and introduced the now much-loved theme "Charity Never Faileth."

When Emmeline approached the beloved composer Evan Stephens to tell him of a poem he might put to music, he took the opportunity to spend an evening visiting in her home with her, and he proposed that she write a song for him to set to music instead. She was a little uncertain, but that same night the words came to her and "Our Mountain Home So Dear" was born. It became one of Evan Stephens' favorites, and a favorite among the Saints.

Emmeline always searched for the heart of things, and the heart of Relief Society she stated in the following words: "We are getting too far away from the spiritual side of our great work, and from the thought that inspired the first organization of Relief Society. The Society stands first for spirituality—and then for charity and mercy."[13]

When Emmeline turned ninety a party was given for her at the Hotel Utah, and two years later more than a thousand people attended her birthday celebration! And she was able to celebrate seeing the nineteenth amendment to the Constitution passed in 1920, allowing voting rights for American women.

Relief Society presidents had always served until death, as did the presidents of the Church and apostles. President Heber J. Grant had hinted at her release, but she would have none of it. But now she was ill and, on April 2, 1921, he came to her home and released her from the sacred calling she had borne so well.

After he left, she suffered a stroke on her way upstairs. After being in a coma for three weeks, she died on April 25, 1921. She was ninety-three years old. The flags flew half-mast in Utah to commemorate her death. Her funeral was one of the largest ever held in the Tabernacle, and the second for a woman.

Honorary degrees were afforded her, and on the hundredth anniversary of her birth, the women of Utah commissioned a marble bust to be placed in the rotunda of the state capitol, reading simply, "A Fine Soul Who Served Us."

Perhaps the most complete, the most intensely beautiful tribute paid to Emmeline B. Wells came from the heart and pen of Susa Young Gates, daughter of Brigham Young:

> Her mind is keen, her intellect sure, and her powers unbending. She possesses a rarely beautiful spirit, and is affectionate, confiding, and exquisitely pure. No unclean thing could enter her presence, or remain in her atmosphere. She is an eloquent speaker, a beautiful writer, a true friend, and a wise counselor.
>
> She is beloved by all who dwell in the Church, and by all who know her, and their name is legion.[14]

ENDNOTES

1. Andrus, "They Knew the Prophet," 156–57.
2. Madsen, *In Their Own Words*, 45.
3. "Wells, EB," *Encyclopedia of Mormonism*, 1559–60. 1992
4. "Emmeline B. Wells," Wikipedia.org/wiki/Emmeline B. Wells, 1 of 3.
5. "Online library details westward trek," *Church News*, Feb. 13, 2003, Archives, thechurchnews.com/archives/2003-02-15/online-library -details-westward-trek-104016.
6. Ibid.
7. Wells, *Defender: The Life of Daniel H. Wells.*
8. "Emmeline B. Wells," Church History Topics; seechurchofjesuschrist .org/study/history/topics/emmeline-b-wells?lang=eng.
9. Gospel Link library document, gospelink.com/library/document 24932?highlight=1, 2 of 5.
10. Carol Cornwall Madsen, "Emmeline B. Wells: A Fine Soul Who Served," *Ensign*, July 2003, churchofjesuschrist.org/study /ensign/2003/07/emmeline-b-wells-a-fine-soul-who-served?lang=eng.
11. Madsen, "Emmeline B. Wells, Romantic Rebel," *Supporting Saints: Life Stories of Nineteenth-Century Mormons*, rsc.byu.edu/supporting -saints-life-stories-nineteenth-century-mormons/emmeline-b-wells.
12. Elaine L. Jack, "Believing in the Light after Darkness," *Heroines of the Restoration*, 167.
13. Mormonwomenstand.com; see mormonwomenstand.com /emmeline-wells/.
14. Susa Young Gates, "President Emmeline B. Wells," *Album Book: Daughters of Utah Pioneers and Their Mothers,* 54.

NAUVOO, ILLINOIS

W hen the Saints, hunted and exhausted, reached the Mississippi River and the end of Missouri, they crossed over into Illinois and were kindly received by the citizens of Quincy, who were moved by their plight and offered them a safe haven. Joseph rejoined his people on April 22, 1839. His presence was a signal for action. The second day after his arrival he called a conference to reorganize the Saints. A committee was given power to purchase farm land from Dr. Galland, who owned large amounts of property in Commerce, Illinois.

Commerce was a swampy wilderness. But the land, covered with trees and bushes, rose to the level of the prairie, rich with grasses, wildflowers, and stands of timber. "Believing that it might become a healthful place by the blessings of Heaven to the Saints . . I considered it wisdom," Joseph stated, "to make an attempt to build up a city."[1]

But this was followed by what seemed to be the usual period of suffering and trial for the Saints. Weakened by the harsh elements and poverty, the Saints were easy targets for the malaria which infested the swamps. Every family was struck to some degree. But Joseph, ill himself, rose up from his sick bed, gathered some of the brethren to go with him, and proceeded to heal the Saints—in Nauvoo, and across the river on the Iowa side. And many miracles occurred that day.

Nauvoo became the largest city in Illinois, with schools, newspapers, theatres, stores and businesses of all variety, its own militia, and thousands of converts pouring in daily to increase the number of faithful Saints. And, yes, there was a second temple in the works. Many of the faithful Saints were being seasoned for the time when Brother Joseph would no longer be with them, when Nauvoo, the beloved City of Joseph, would also be ravaged and left behind, and their last journey would be one that covered vast wilderness—unknown, unexplored, uncivilized—but sanctified by the thousands of feet that trod the desert and mountain wastes to the Valley of the Great Salt Lake, the final promised land.

ENDNOTE

1. Joseph Smith, in B. H. Roberts, *A Comprehensive History of the Church,* 2:9.

SARAH MELISSA GRANGER KIMBALL

SARAH WAS BORN IN THE village of Phelps, New York, just scant miles away from Palmyra, four days after Christmas, in the year 1818. The Book of Mormon found its way to her father only months after its publication in 1830, and Oliver Granger had no chance, really, to turn it away, for a vision was vouchsafed him in which "Moroni told him that it was a 'true record of great worth.'" In Sarah's words, "He also promised my father that he might ask for what he most desired and it would be granted. He asked for an evidence by which he might know when he was approved of God. The evidence, or sign, was given, and remained with him until his dying hour, being more particularly manifest when engaged in prayer and meditation. I love the memory of my father."[1]

This vision had a consummate effect on eleven-year-old Sarah, and helped to create a true testimony within her.[2]

The family was baptized, and in 1833 moved to Kirtland. Sarah was still in her teens, but she was one of only twenty-three women who attended Joseph's School of the Prophets which was first held there; Sarah, it is noted, attended the Hebrew school. This may be thought of as nothing but a fact in passing, but with the bright intelligence of Sarah's mind and spirit, she learned much. Her understanding was opened, her desires quickened, and her faith made more sure.

Kirtland was a paradox, a scene of opposites and confusion. There was a brief spell of peace, with the Spirit of the Lord like a shield and a comforter round the Saints, with the blessings of the temple, of angels, of heavenly visitors. But greed and speculation, the spirit of dissension, and at last an apostasy became so terrible that the Prophet Joseph, Brigham Young, and others had to flee for their lives.

All this played upon the mind of the serious young woman, whose family remained so stalwart that Joseph sent Sarah's father, Oliver, to return to Kirtland in an attempt to settle some of the debts of the Church yet remaining there.

The Prophet Joseph, knowing the hearts of his people through the power of the Spirit, made promises to Brother Granger—but also to Sarah at this time, promises "that were very sacred and very comforting to her throughout her life."[3]

In 1831 Sarah's first son, Hiram, was born. She was to give birth to two more sons, Oliver Granger and Franklin D. Kimball. Later, in the Salt Lake Valley, the Indian agent gave Sarah "a nine-year-old wild Indian girl" she adopted and raised.[4]

Sarah certainly possessed a bold and lively sense of humor, illustrated by the following story from her autobiography in the *Woman's Exponent* in 1883:

Sarah's husband, Hiram, was not a member of the Church when she first married him in Nauvoo, but he knew how deeply committed and converted she was to the Mormon faith. When her little son was born, they were both enchanted with him and, as he was admiring his three-day old child, Sarah said, "'What is the boy worth?' He replied, 'I don't know; he is worth a great deal.' I said, 'Is he worth a thousand dollars?' The reply was, 'Yes, more than that if he lives and does well.' I said, 'Half of him is mine, is it not?' 'Yes, I suppose so.' 'Then I have something to help on the Temple'" (pleasantly).

"'You have?' 'Yes, and I think of turning my share right in as tithing.' 'Well, I'll think about that.' Hiram went to see Brother Joseph to see what he thought of this tithing donation. Joseph accepted the child readily and offered that Hiram give the child to the church immediately for $500. or keep the child for a $500. donation. Hiram asked if he could donate land instead, which again, was readily accepted."[5]

Following this experience, Joseph Smith said to Sarah: "You have consecrated your first born, for this you are blessed of the Lord. I bless you in the name of the Lord God of Abraham, Isaac, and Jacob, and I seal upon you all the blessings that pertain to the faithful. Your name shall be handed down in honorable remembrance from generation to generation."[6]

While her husband was going about his affairs, making money, dealing with the world, the Nauvoo Sarah lived in was not a quiet place. Danger was a constant undertone, for the Saints, as well as for the Prophet Joseph. There was progress; the city offered schools, a university, theatres, thriving businesses, and a constant influx of converts from across the ocean.

But running through everything that was happening was the constant need to finish the temple, where covenants with the Lord would offer strength, understanding, and protection to the Saints.

The temple walls were only three feet high, and it was imperative that the work go forth. Women were already helping, doing what they could, but there was no sense of organization. There had been a great appeal for clothing and provisions for the workmen. Sarah's seamstress, Miss Cook, expressed her willingness to sew if the cloth could just be provided. Sarah said she could help with that—and perhaps there were other women who were willing to assist, or to provide materials, women who felt much as they felt.

Perhaps they could organize a sewing society! They invited about a dozen women to Sarah Kimball's house on the following Thursday, and the subject was enthusiastically approved. Sister Rigdon suggested that they involve Eliza R. Snow and ask her to draw up a constitution and by-laws for the fledgling association. She enthusiastically, and beautifully, did so, and they anxiously presented their ideas and efforts to the Prophet.

And this is where heaven stepped in. "This is not what you want," he told them. "There is something better for you. I have desired to organize the sisters in the order of the Priesthood. I now have the key by which I can do it."

He further added, "Tell the sisters their offering is accepted of the Lord, and he has something better for them than a written constitution. I invite them all to meet with me and a few of the brethren . . . next Thursday afternoon, and I will organize the women under the priesthood after the pattern of the priesthood."[7]

The women were ready. They had made their own efforts, expressed their willingness. Their hearts and their spirits were open. Then Joseph made that powerful, well-known statement: "The organization of the Church of Christ was never perfect until the women were thus organized."[8]

It is interesting that Sarah sought no honor or position for herself. When the officers were chosen, she was not among them, but her understanding and commitment kept her safely in the midst of the work.

Sarah's husband was facing financial challenges during the period when the Prophet was slain and the Saints were busily preparing for the journey West. So Sarah found herself remaining in Nauvoo when the main body left, one wagon after another. She watched her friends go, but she seemed to have a quiet assurance that all would be well with her.

She corresponded with her friend Marinda Hyde, wife of Orson Hyde. In one letter she wrote: "Nothing affords me more pleasure than to be assured that I am not forgotten by one whome I so dearly love. Dear Sister H, you must have had yr heart and hands full, but you say you had strength given according to yr day, inasmuch as you have not been overcome. It is all right, for your husband said when here that we *must overcome all things* in order to become pillars in the Temple of God. The desire of your friend and Sister is that we, with all that pertains to us, may be prepared to become strong pillars in the Temple of our God."[9]

Sarah did leave Nauvoo, traveling with her two sons, her widowed mother, two of her brothers, and a young girl who lived nine years with Sarah. They arrived safely in the Salt Lake Valley in September of 1851. Her husband was still in New York City, but when he came to join her at last, he was a broken man.

But Sarah had already taken matters in hand, purchasing "a comfortable little home"[10] with the money she received from selling the outfit with which she had traveled West. Then she began teaching school in the 14th Ward, and was able to sustain her family.

When she bore her last son she resigned from teaching, but only for three months. "I said to my husband, 'If you and the little boys will go to the canon and get some timber we can build a schoolroom' . . . by a great deal of faith and exertion on (my) part and diligent labor by (my) husband and sons it was accomplished."[11]

In 1857 Sarah was called to be president of her 15th Ward Relief Society. This honored post she held and magnified until her death in 1898, over forty years later.

Sarah had her teaching, her three sons, and the three adopted daughters. One of these was Kate, "a nine-year-old wild Indian girl whom I educated and raised."[12] Kate, sadly, died at nineteen.

Sarah was a conscientious mother. To her daughter, Lizzie, she wrote: "In blessing others, we are blessed. Let us continue our labors of love as God shall give us strength."[13]

In 1861 Sarah's mother, who had lived with her for twenty years, died. In 1863 Sarah's husband, on his way to serve a mission in the Sandwich Islands, was drowned in the Pacific Ocean by the wreck of the steamer, *Ada Hancock,* off the coast of San Pedro. He was only sixty-two years old.

Sorrow followed sorrow, but this one involved the fact that Sarah was now a widow, with the entire weight of sustaining her family upon her shoulders only. She was to remain a widow for the next thirty-five years.

In 1865 Sarah records only that another little girl was brought to her, whom she adopted. And the work went on. In 1868, through much vision, determination, and faith, the sisters of the Fifteenth Ward dedicated their completed Relief Society building whose upper story would be "dedicated to art and to science; the lower story to commerce or trade."[14]

This was a monumental accomplishment. Sarah held an expanded vision of women and Relief Society, and she urged the sisters to come to the meetings "prepared to entertain each other with reading, speaking, or singing, and not spend all the time in work." She also urged them to learn physiology so that they might take care of their bodies as well as their inner, or spiritual selves.[15]

Sarah, too, was an advocate of women's rights. After she was called as secretary of the general Relief Society, under Eliza R. Snow, she became more actively involved in this cause, and knew and worked with Susan B. Anthony and other prominent leader. Susa Young Gates wrote of Sarah: "(Eliza R. Snow) turned over the active direction of this suffrage movement to that champion of equal rights, Sarah M. Kimball. For many years, Mrs. Kimball was the 'Mormon' suffrage standard bearer. It would be less than justice if it were not here recorded that her active brain, her unselfish devotion to the work of God, and her magnificent organizing powers, bore rich fruit during this vital period, (1868-1893) in the history of women's development in the Church."[16]

Sarah's understanding of spiritual matters was deeply comprehensive, as was her desire to love and lift and enlighten her sisters, in the Church, and beyond.

Just three years before her death she presented a profound, significant paper at the Triennial Council of Women in Washington, D.C. in February 1895. She entitled the paper "Our Sixth Sense, or the Sense of Spiritual Understanding." With tender boldness, she spoke from the depths of her own heart:

"The sixth sense links mortal with immortal existence. . . . It educates, exalts and refines those that heed its whisperings, and follow its guiding influence. This sense leads to blissful heights of superior understanding. . . . It illumines the soul that cultivates it; purifies thoughts and actions; enlarges the sphere of comprehension, and exalts the aspirations. Its continual exercise brings its possessor nearer and nearer to the throne of the Almighty."

Sarah bears her testimony, and reveals in her words, her demeanor, and her example, the high, holy standard by which she had lived her own life:

> The legitimate exercise of spiritual power . . . puts the individual in possession of keys of knowledge and clothes him with additional responsibility relating to the enlightenment and elevation of the human family. . . .
>
> When through our spiritual nature we are in communication with God, we are drawing nearer and nearer to each other, and our words and works will blend more and more harmoniously, until earth's dutiful children, recognizing universal spiritual kinship, hail the peaceful millennial dawn, and participate in the triumphant reign of our God and His Christ.[17]

ENDNOTES

1. Kimball, "Auto-biography," *Woman's Exponent,* 51.
2. Ibid.
3. Wells, "President Sarah M. Kimball," 116.
4. Turley, *Women of Faith,* 116.
5. As quoted in Relief Society Women, Jan Tolman, September 1, 2008, reliefsocietywomen.com/blog.
6. Kimball, ibid.
7. *Daughters in My Kingdom,* 12–13.
8. Madsen, *In Their Own Words,* 191–92.
9. Turley, 120.
10. Kimball, ibid.
11. Kimball, ibid.
12. Turley, 116.
13. Ibid., 123.
14. Ibid., 125.
15. Turley, 125–26.
16. Gates, "Suffrage Won by the Mothers of the United States," 263.17.
17. Kimball, "Our Sixth Sense, or the Spiritual Understanding," 251.

PATTY BARTLETT SESSIONS

From small things and quiet beginnings, great things can at times come to pass. Patty Bartlett was born on February 4, 1795. Her parents were Enoch and Martha Anna Hall Bartlett, who had settled in the wilderness of Maine where the heavily wooded country was sparsely settled. Her father's first wife, Eliza, bore ten children and died when her youngest child was but nine years old. Yet just four years later, Patty became the first child of her mother, Enoch's second wife, who bore nine children herself and, despite the rigorous, punishing circumstances of her existence, lived past her one hundredth birthday![1]

This stalwart spirit and constitution were passed on to her daughter—as we shall easily see!

"Years later, on 24th June 1863 in Salt Lake City, Patty recorded, 'got my web (woven fabric) out for blanket & undergarments 28 yds I do feel thankful to my heavenly Father that he gives me health and strength and a disposition to work and make cloth and other things for my comfort now in the sixty ninth year of my life. And I also feel thankful that I had a mother that put me to work when I was young and learned me how.'"[2]

Though her parents firmly disapproved of the match, Patty married David Sessions when she was only seventeen years old. They moved ten miles away to be near his parents. His mother, suffering severe rheumatism, needed constant care.

Mother Sessions was, however, a self-taught midwife in the area, and one night a messenger came entreating "young Mrs. Sessions" to come at once, for a young woman was dying. Knowing the time it would take for her mother-in-law to reach the place, Patty did as she was bid. With the courage of necessity, Patty delivered the child and put the mother to bed. When the doctor arrived and assessed the situation, he was greatly impressed by the natural skill of the inexperienced young woman.

The doctor congratulated her, and urged her to continue in this profession, "not to have any fear, for she would prosper in it."³ And thus it was, and thus it continued for the rest of her life.

The Mormon missionaries came to the area in 1833, and Patty wished at once to join the Church, but waited a while to appease her husband, who did not share her convictions. She was baptized in July 1834. Brigham Young and some of the Twelve visited the area in August of the next year, urging the family to gather with the Saints in Missouri. Her husband was at length baptized, and they made the long trip to Missouri, by wagon and on foot.

By this time Patty had given birth to seven children, but four of them had died. She was, however, pregnant at the time of the journey. She was also forty-two years old, displaying the stamina that would be her hallmark throughout her life.

They were not able to settle long in Missouri. A brief year later violence broke out and increased like wildfire, until Governor Boggs issued his infamous Extermination Order, and the Saints, many of them gathered briefly in Far West, were despoiled of all their goods and hounded out of the state.

It was winter, and the people were poorly prepared to walk through deep snows and ice-encrusted rivers, or cold mud that sucked at their shoes and boots. Little Amanda, Patty's youngest, remained sick for most of the journey, no matter how Patty tried to keep her fed and warm. She did not survive the ordeal, but died in Nauvoo in May of 1841 of croup, at the age of three.

A fact on a sheet. But how Patty had labored and yearned over this little one. Now, out of eight children, she had only three left.

Her married son Perrigrine left for a year-long mission to Maine, and her husband, Mr. Sessions, as she called him, began building a house. It was established that her family, husband and son, had lost twelve hundred dollars in land and four hundred dollars in livestock and corn when they were driven from Missouri.⁴

Survival now, and beginning anew, was a daunting task. But basically all of the Saints faced the same ordeal together, and aided one another, and constantly expressed their gratitude to God and their faith. Without the strength of these qualities they would not have survived Missouri, nor what they would soon face in Nauvoo.

During this period Patty was sealed to Joseph Smith, in March of 1842. Willard Richards performed the ceremony, which became and remained the most sacred portion of her life in the long struggles ahead.

Patty continued her midwifing. As expressed in one *Woman's Exponent* account, "She helped to lay out the dead, and she officiated in her calling as a midwife. On one occasion she froze her hands and toes as she went through severe weather to attend to a sick woman. In August of 1842 she attended the birth of a stillborn baby, her first such event, she indicated, 'in thirty years of midwifery.'"[5]

Patty became one of the first members of the Nauvoo Relief Society and through this association with the wives of the leading brethren, close friendships grew. This lifelong circle of friends Patty later referred to as "Brigham's girls" or "Heber's girls," perhaps because many of these women were, in fact, married to Church leaders, particularly Brigham and Heber.[6]

When Joseph and Hyrum Smith were killed by the mob in Carthage Jail, all of Nauvoo was stunned with an anguish of grief and dismay. How could they go on without the presence and the love of the Prophet? The *Exponent* records: "Suffice it to say that Sister Sessions suffered with the people in sacrificing her home, etc., and also mourned much in her own breast, for she had the most profound admiration and respect for him as a Prophet of God."[7]

Again it was a small thing that led to something great and immeasurably valuable. While living in Nauvoo a friend simply gave Patty a little notebook. What moved her to start a record of her life? At the beginning she wrote: "A Day book given to me Patty Sessions by Sylvia P. Lyon this 10th day of Feb. 1846 Patty Sessions her Book I am now fifty-one years six days old February 10 1846 City of Joseph Hancock Co Ill."

She began to keep a diary, and she wrote everything that came to her mind, from her feelings and frustrations, to the happenings of those with whom she was closely associated, to the daily routines and doings of her own life.

Patty and David received their endowments in the Nauvoo Temple in 1846. Perigrene helped his parents prepare for the journey, and they left in February of 1846.

From her writings it is easy to tell the sense of confusion and uncertainty that characterized those first few weeks, and even months. There was much running back to get something left behind, or to buy horses or oxen. Organizations were still being put together, and men appointed captains of hundreds, fifties, and tens.

Perhaps the first leg was the hardest, getting used to everything. On Thursday, March 5, Patty writes: "Put John Joens wife to bed mis carriage we start along Mr. Sessions has lost sight of the cow I have to drive while he goes to hunt for her . . . it is so late we do not pitch our tent travel 13 miles. Friday 6 I go back ten miles this morning to see Sarah Ann Whitney she is sick sent for me I rode horse back she was better when I got there and I drove her carriage in to the camp in the after noon with her and her mother the camp did not start to day. Our horse was sick last night but they laid hands on him and he is better to day."

Bits and snatches from the last week in the month are quite grim: "rains and snows very cold and muddy stay in the wagon," "snows cold nothing for our teams to eat yesterday nor this morning but brows" (brows are the tender shoots and twigs of trees and shrubs), "cold wind blows hard our tent down every little while."

April does not seem much better. Patty simply remarks on the sixth: "The church 15 years old to day it rains hard." A delightful addition makes one smile: On that same day she records, "Br Brigham came up with his company driving his team in the rain and mud to his knes—happy as a king."

She writes how she sits and cries when she learns that her children, whom she thought were coming, are not. She is ill, more than once, recording on Monday, June 15, "I am truly sick can neither eat nor sleep."[8]

She notes how several of her friends, more than once, take her clothes and wash them for her, refusing remuneration—for has she not on many occasions tended and nursed them, and even saved their lives?

During this period Patty suffered greatly in trying to deal with a second wife David had taken, Rosella, who had refused to come West, then appeared all of a sudden with the determination to lure Patty's husband back to Nauvoo with her. She was insolent and lazy, refusing to do any sort of work, but willing to take advantage of those who labored hard. It broke Patty's heart and it drove her half-mad to deal with the woman, but at length Rosella disappeared much as she had come, and became little more than a shadow upon the surface of Patty's life.

There were times that were lovely and magical. But Patty's work seemed always to be somehow woven into the fabric of her days. In February of 1847 she records:

> Thursday 4 my birthday fifty two years old . . . we had brandy and drank a toast to each other desireing and wishing the blesings of God to be with us all and that we might live and do all that we came here into this world to do. Eliza Snow came here after me to go to a little party in the evening. I was glad to see her told her it was my birth day and she must bless me she said if I would go to the party they all would bless me I then went and put James Bulloch wife to bed (with a daughter) then went to the party had a good time singing praying speaking in tounges before we broke up I was called away to sister Morse then to sister Whitney then back to sister Morse put her to bed 2 oclock, with a son.[9]

In June 1847 the "Big Company" was preparing to leave Winter Quarters at last. On Friday the fourth Patty writes:

> We do not go to day Mr. Sessions and I went to Br. Leonards to a party we had a feast of good things both temporal and spiritual when going there I called to sister Kimbals and with E. R. Snow blessed Helen and Genette then in the gift of tongues E. R. Snow sung a blessing to all the rest of the girls. Saturday 5 we start for the mount ains and leave winter Quarters (for the) mountains or a resting place ten years to day since we left our home in Maine we now leave many good friends I hope will soon follow on to us I drive one four ox team go 4 miles camp.

As they traveled, Patty saw antelope, hundreds of buffalo, dead Indians, dead white men, unfriendly Indians, burned out Indian villages, and many strange sights. The travelers somehow maintained a sense of a normal routine, which especially included meetings, and times of helping one another, with songs, prayers, speaking in tongues, and literal blessings.

On September 24 the Valley was reached at last. This was the first group to reach the Salt Lake Valley after the initial settlement in July. Several of Patty's children with their families came West in this same rather loose organization.

Patty's journal tells of these important first days. On September 24 she wrote: "The valley is a beautiful place my heart flows with gratitude to god that we have got home all safe lost nothing have been blessed with life and health I rejoice all the time. The following day: I have drove my wagon all the way but part of the two last mts . . . I broke nothing nor turned over had good luck. I have cleaned my wagon and myself and visited some old friends."

On Sunday the 26th she wrote: "Go to meeting hear the epistle read from the twelve then went put Lorenzo Youngs wife Harriet to bed with a son (Lorenzo Dow, Jr.) *the first male born in this valley it was said to me more than 5 months ago that my hands should be the first to handle the first born son in the place of rest for the saints even in the city of our God I have come more than one thousand miles to do it since it was spoken.*"[10]

Patty prospered in the Valley, and was as restlessly busy as ever. She delivered roughly 250 babies her first year, and was said to have delivered in her lifetime just shy of 4,000. She was always interested in the less fortunate which, in Utah, applied to the native Indian tribes.

Her husband, David, died in 1850, when Patty was in her mid-fifties. She did not stay unmarried long. John Parry, a gifted musician from Wales who became the first conductor of the Tabernacle Choir, arrived in the Valley in 1851 and asked Patty to marry him. His wife, Mary, had died of cholera in Council Bluffs.

She had a man again to do some of the things, such as chopping wood, that were most difficult for her. Patty moved easily into her now-accustomed role of bearing most of the household responsibilities, continuing her midwifing, taking in borders, doing much of her cooking and cleaning, and even the bookkeeping that her work entailed. She had a canny sense for good business and turned everything she touched into a profit, amassing by 1883 $16,000 worth of shares in ZCMI (Zion's Cooperative Mercantile Institute).

At the beginning of 1865, when she was approaching seventy, Patty wrote at the heading of the new year: "I enjoy health and activity can go and assotiate with my children and their children and their children's children."

Patty taught her children prayer and urged them to teach their own the same, from the very littlest on up. She believed in faith, in service, in giving to any and all of the causes of the Lord's work. She always gave freely to the Perpetual Emigration Fund. On April 15, 1863, she recorded "I gave him, Presd=Young, seventy-five Dollars for the missionaries. I have put in five Dollars before all gold and silver. And twenty five pounds dried peaches. And ten pounds dried peaches and three and a half yards of sheeting. To those that go after the saints to the Missouri River."

The following August 11th she wrote: "I gave two thousand three hundred and fifty pounds of flour for the building of the new tabernacle."[11]

She bought horses, land and house lots, made sure her wheat brought good prices, kept meticulous records, and was interested in loss and profit. Yet, this following instance is not unusual: "Nov=16 1863 Naomi debenham came here to stay a few days to rest her. She was a stranger to me I never saw her before she said she was tired out and full of grief she had buried her Brother the day before. She took very sick the Doctors were here to see her one said she could not live. But by the faith of the saints and the power of the priesthood and good nursing she got well. On December 12th she adds: "She left here but not able to pay any thing for her trouble she was here four weeks lacking two days."[12]

At the end of 1866 Patty's journal becomes very fragmentary for a period, until it picks up again in mid-1880. John Parry died in 1868. One of the last entries concerning him is Friday 28 of December: "Mr. Parry sick he sent for me I went to see him" and Saturday, very briefly, "he is better."[13] John had married two wives following his marriage to Patty: Grace Williams, sister to his first wife, Mary, and Harried Parry, a cousin.

Parry had been asked by Brigham Young to organize a choir, which later became the Tabernacle Choir. Parry himself had a beautiful singing voice, but of this portion of her husband's life, Patty makes no mention. She does say at his death on June 13, 1868: "Mr. Parry died he has been sick over a year Suffered more than tongue can tell. In all his sickness he was patient more so than any person I ever saw. I never heard a murmur from his lips. Died without a struggle or a groan. A good man. A kind husband a tender Father and a good Latter-day Saint."[14]

Many of Patty's entries at this time concern the expenditure of her monies, and it is interesting to see the price she paid for various commodities. For instance, in April 1864, she paid $130 for a yoke of oxen—"to send to the states to bring the poor saints on."[15] She bought a mare for $220, a stove for $185, and a farm from her son David for $1860.

She was constantly giving, donating, to dozens of people and causes.

In May of 1870 when Patty was seventy-five years old, she went on a journey with her son Perrigren, and many others, to visit Maine, and hopefully to see relatives she hadn't seen for over thirty-four years. On May 13 she records: "We started for our visit, had a pleasant journey not sick one day while we were gone. and I never tasted tea nor coffee while I was gone. I drank cold water. And it was my meat and my drink and I know it is good for me to let those things alone that we were told it is not good for us. (Word of Wisdom) We got home."

In August she adds just a little more, putting, as always, the cost! "This journey cost me over 500 Dollars but I do not Regret going I have seen my friends and Bore a faithful testimony to them wherever I went of the truth of the Latter-day work called Mormonism."[16]

On December 4, 1872, Patty left Salt Lake and moved to Bountiful. She had a house built in this city, which her son Perrigrine was largely responsible for founding. She was giving more and more, to every conceivable Church cause, to help many members of her family who were in need of money for one reason or another, and to build a Patty Sessions Academy for her grandchildren and for those who would otherwise be unable to obtain an education. This lovely brick school was free for all. Even though Patty was eighty-eight years old, she taught some of the classes.

She was interminably sewing and knitting, most of the things she made intended as gifts for others. In fact, her last entry, covering the first few days of May 1888, reads: "I have knit & the most of the time three pair of stockings this week it is now Friday the 4th. She dries prodigious amounts of fruit from her peach trees and, in 1886 reads the Book of Mormon all the way through."

By now Patty was well into her nineties. She still wrote of getting in the corn, hauling and stacking it. In an entry at age ninety-three "she speaks of going for sleigh rides nearly every day and clearing snow off her house after a storm."[17]

She did not know how to stop, or how to live without giving. She understood the powerful interrelatedness of the Saints and of the women in particular. She had seen, and was part of, how the kingdom works, and how the power that moves it is the power of love. She died in 1892 at the age of ninety-seven.

Throughout her life the indomitable spirit flourished, no matter how the body might have suffered. From time to time Patty bore her testimony to her children:

I gave liberally. I have done these things with a willing heart and hand and the Lord has blessed me. . . He has blessed me with the enjoyment of his holy spirit which has comforted my heart in every time of need. And I have to say to my Grand children and great Grand children. Be faithful in paying your tithing, your fast donations. And responding to every call made by the Authorities of the Church . . . Be faithful in your Prayers in your families. Do right let the result follow. And the Lord will bless you with wisdom, knowledge, and intelligence. Riches. Honor, and every good thing that your hearts can desire in righteousness.[18]

She spoke truly, and she lived truly, as testimony of her words.

ENDNOTES

1. Sessions, *Mormon Midwife: The 1846–1888 Diaries of Patty Bartlett Sessions,* 2.
2. Ibid., 5–6, quoted in "Patty Sessions," *Woman's Exponent* 13 (1 September): 51.
3. Ibid., 6.
4. Sessions, 19.
5. Ibid., 22.
6. Karras, *More than Petticoats: Remarkable Utah Women,* 4.
7. "Patty Sessions," *Woman's Exponent* 13 (1 February): 135. As quoted in Diaries of Patty Bartlett Sessions, 23.
8. Diary entries, date as noted.
9. Sessions, 71.
10. Diary entry, date as noted.
11. Sessions, 345.
12. Ibid., 345–46.
13. Sessions, 338.
14. Ibid., 346.
15. Ibid.
16. Ibid., 348.
17. Karras, 9.
18. Sessions, 342. See also page 3 of her own Diary #7.

AMANDA BARNES SMITH

LIFE OFTEN CONTAINS ELEMENTS OF truth that are strange and almost unbelievable. We live them, scarcely comprehending what we are going through. Amanda's life was a powerful example of the wonder and inconceivability of this statement.

Amanda was born on February 22, 1809, in Becket, Massachusetts. During most of her childhood, however, the family lived in Amherst, Ohio. At the young age of seventeen, in the year 1826, she married Warren Smith, even though her parents were opposed to the marriage. Warren was a blacksmith, but he was also fifteen years older than Amanda. However, there was also another situation that sent danger signals to her parents, and ought to have concerned her as well.

Warren, at his own admission, was in love with another woman, to whom he had been engaged before, but the couple had somehow become estranged. He told Amanda that he loved her (Amanda), but he also struggled with love for this other woman. "I love her little finger more than I love your whole body," he said.[1]

In the area of Amherst there was a Campbellite movement with a very compelling preacher by the name of Sidney Rigdon. Amanda was drawn to his preaching—so much so that three years later, when she heard missionaries preach the restored gospel, she was baptized on the first day of April 1831. Her husband was more hesitant, but he did join the Church a little later.

Conversion always brought change, for the new members had to leave their present home in order to join with the Saints and live in the society of those who believed as they did. In 1837 they left Amherst and traveled to Kirtland, Ohio. Kirtland was lovely. They lived close to the temple, and the Prophet was there. But the failure of the Kirtland Safety Society, and the speculation that was rampant, had its effect on Warren, though in 1838 they left Kirtland to join with the rest of the Saints in northern Missouri.

They had no idea what they would find there; they went eagerly, and with faith. It was spring, and the traveling was better than it might have been. It was an eight-hundred-mile journey to Missouri, and on the way they stopped at Amherst to say goodbye to their family and friends there.

"We visited our friends in Amherst but the treatment that we received will never be forgot(t) en by me," Amanda wrote. "My mother said she hoped she would never see me or her of me nor hear my name mentioned again. But we bid them good by (e) and left them."[2]

This set a very sad tone for their journey, and as they neared the end of their ordeal they were stunned and horrified when a mob of armed men rode up and stopped them, threatening that "if we went another step they would kill us all."

There were nine wagons in their company, and all were held under guard for three days. Imagine, if we can, what those three days were like. Amanda says: "I thought is this our boasted land of liberty, for some said, we must deny our faith, or they would kill us; others said, we should die at any rate."[3]

They traveled ten miles after they were released, then arrived in Haun's Mill, which Amanda describes as "a small town, composed of one grist mill, one saw mill, and eight or ten houses, belonging to our brethren."[4]

They stopped there, intending to spend the night. But just before sunset a mob of three hundred—*three hundred men*—burst upon them, and the men yelled for the women and children to run for the woods. Many of the mob "came like so many demons or wild Indians," shooting at the men who were trying to hide in the blacksmith's shop, firing, too, at the helpless women and little children, heading for the creek and the bottom land beyond.

Amanda had escaped with her two daughters, but when at last the murderers left, she returned to see old Brother McBride, dead and mangled. When her own oldest son emerged from the blacksmith shop he was carrying little Alma, and had to tell his mother that her husband and her other son had been killed.

What happened next can only be told in Amanda's words:

> I could not weep then. The fountain of tears was dry . . . and all the
> mother's sense absorbed in its anxiety for the precious boy which God

alone could save by his miraculous aid. The entire hip joint had been shot away. Flesh, bone, joint had been ploughed out from the muzzle of the gun which the ruffian placed to the child's hip through the logs of the shop and deliberately fired. We laid little Alma on a bed in our tent and examined the wound. It was a ghastly sight. I knew not what to do.[5]

It was now night. Amid the women and children sobbing for their losses, and wounded men moaning in their pain, Amanda turned to "God as our physician and help."

> *"Oh my Heavenly Father," I cried, "what shall I do? Thou seest my poor wounded boy and knowest my inexperience. Oh, Heavenly Father, direct me what to do!"*

And then I was directed as though by a voice speaking to me. The ashes of our fire was still smouldering. We had been burning the bark of the shag-bark hickory. I was directed to take those ashes and make a lye and put a cloth saturated with it right into the wound. It hurt, but little Alma was so near dead to heed it much. Again and again I saturated the cloth and put it into the hole from which the hip joint had been ploughed, and each time mashed flesh and splinters of bone came away with the cloth; and the wound became as white as chicken's flesh.

Having done as directed I again prayed to the Lord and *was again instructed as distinctly as though a physician had been standing by speaking to me.* Near by was a slippery elm tree. From this I was told to make a slippery-elm poultice and fill the wound with it. . . the wound which took fully a quarter of a yard of linen to cover, so large was it, was properly dressed.

It was then I found vent to my feelings in tears, and resigned myself to the anguish of the hour. And all that night we, a few poor, stricken women, were thus left there with our dead and wounded. All through the night we heard the groans of the dying.[6]

Brother Joseph Young arrived the following morning, but he was so horrified that he scarcely knew what to do. They had not time to bury the dead, for fear of the mob, so placed them as carefully as possible into an empty well—all thrown in together, and covered with earth and straw.

Alma was suffering greatly, but Amanda found some balsam to help ease the pain. She describes what happened next:

> "Alma, my child," I said, "you believe that the Lord made your hip?"
> "Yes, Mother."

"Well, the Lord can make something there in the place of your hip, don't you believe that he can, Alma?"

"Do you think the Lord can, Mother?"

"Yes, my son," I replied. "He has shown it all to me in a vision."

Alma was required to lay on his face, and move as little as possible—which he did for five long weeks! And a gristle of some sorts grew up where the joint and socket had been, and Alma walked—without a limp, without any aid, for the rest of his life.[7]

The women left behind there held little prayer meetings, but the mobsters said they would kill every one of them if they did not stop. They tried little spelling schools for their children, but were told the same thing. Amanda could not bear it! She records:

> I stole down to a corn field, and crawled into a stalk of corn. It was as the temple of the Lord to me at that moment. I prayed aloud and most fervently. *When I emerged from the corn a voice spoke to me. It was a voice as plain as I ever heard one. It was no silent, strong impression of the spirit, but a voice, repeating a verse of the Saints' hymn:*

> *That soul who on Jesus hath leaded for repose,*
> *I cannot, I will not, desert to his foes;*
> *That soul, though all hell should endeavor to shake,*
> *I'll never, no never, no never forsake"*

> From that moment I had no more fear. I felt that nothing could hurt me. Soon after the mob sent word that unless we were all out of the State by a certain day we should be killed. The day came, and at evening came *fifty armed men* to execute the sentence. I met them at the door—I bade them enter and see their own work. They crowded into my room and I showed them my wounded boy. They came party after party, until all had seen my excuse.

> At last they went away, all but two. These I thought were detailed to kill us. "Madam," said one, "have you any meat in the house?" "No," was my reply. "Could you dress a fat hog if one was laid at your door?" "I think we could!" was my answer.[8]

The men who had come to murder them brought the meat. And in time Alma recovered enough that they might think of leaving the state—save for the fact that the mob had taken her horses, beeves, hogs, and wagons.

With an indomitable courage born of faith, Amanda went ten miles into Daviess County and demanded of Captain Comstock her horses. One of them she saw right there in his yard. He requested five dollars for its keep, knowing, of course, that she had no money.

"I did not fear the captain of the mob," she stated. "For I had the Lord's promise that nothing should hurt me."[9]

At length she went into Comstock's yard and took her horse. Then, learning that her other horse was at the mill, she yoked a pair of steers to a sled, drove to the mill, and demanded her second horse also. "Comstock was there at the mill," she recorded. "He gave me the horse, and then asked if I had any flour. 'No; we have had none for weeks.' He then gave me about fifty pounds of flour and some beef, and filled a can with honey."[10]

It angered her to receive small "gifts" from the store of goods which had been stolen from herself and the others! But she was providentially protected, and the Lord kept His word to His faithful handmaiden, who had appealed to Him in faith.

Once Alma walked and was up from his sickbed, Amanda packed her wagon and headed across the Mississippi River to Commerce, which became Nauvoo. "I drove my own team and slept out of doors. We suffered very much from cold, huger and fatigue."[11]

Amanda had no money when she left, and was going through enemy territory, but in time she arrived safely and began at once to teach school, that she might have some means of supplying the needs of her four small children.

Amanda remarried very quickly after arriving with the Saints, needing the companionship and help marriage would provide. The man she married was a blacksmith named Warren Smith—all exactly like her first husband! For only a time was the marriage a happy one, but she remained with him, even after learning that he was involved with another woman and had two children by her.

Amanda had four children by her first husband and three by her second. Earlier, after the birth of her second child, the doctors told her she must not try to have more children. But when the Mormon missionaries came they gave her a blessing, stating that there were other children still waiting to come to her. She claimed to have had no pains when her twins were born, and knew this was a blessing from the Lord.

Now all that was behind her; so much was behind her. She went on. She went forward. She bent her heart and her energies upon those things that mattered most. In July 1842, only three women were chosen to go in person to petition Governor Carlin: Emma Smith, Eliza R. Snow, and Amanda Smith. Their petition, and the facts they presented, made no difference; the dye had already been cast.

Amanda was frustrated by the nature of the two men to whom she had been married, and she liked not the fact that she was unsealed for the eternities to come. Expressing this deep concern to Brigham Young, he replied, "I'll tell you what to do, will you do it?" She assented, and Brigham said, "Choose a proxy and be sealed to Joseph." And so she did.[12]

Struggling for the means to go West, Amanda and her family traveled as far as Keosauqua, Iowa, where she gave birth to her last child, Sarah, on September 10, 1846. It was not until 1850 that they finally made the journey to Utah.

But the year ended in divorce, the end of this second marriage. "He went overboard," Amanda wrote. "I left him and took my children and began to do for myself."[13]

Amanda settled in the Salt Lake Twelfth Ward and stayed there for the thirty-six remaining years of her life. Amanda helped to organize the first Relief Society in Salt Lake, and was called as assistant secretary of the general organization in 1854.[14]

The Lord allowed her to be tried sorely, but He also blessed her abundantly.

Amanda bore a testimony that yet remains a powerful example of a daughter of God who lived her life in obedience, gratitude, and faith:

> I have drank the bitter dregs of the cup of sorrow and affliction, as well as partaken of the blessing of an all merciful God. I have drank from the fountain of the waters of life freely. I have seen the Lord's power manifest to a great degree. I have seen the lame leap as an hart, the eyes of the blind open, and as it were, the dead raised to life—all in my own family since I have been a member of the Church of Jesus Christ. . . . I feel that of all women I have the greatest reason to rejoice and thank my Heavenly Father; and I do thank and praise his holy name for his blessings to me; and I do desire that I may ever be kept faithful unto the end that I may receive the reward of the just.[15]

ENDNOTES

1. Turley, *Women of Faith in the Latter Days*, 330.
2. Ibid., 331.
3. *History of the Church*, 1838–1856, volume C-1 (2 November 1838–31 July 1842).
4. Ibid., 1.
5. Tullidge, *The Women of Mormondom*, eremita.di.uminho.pt/gutenberg /5/4/3/3/54335/54335-h/54335-h.htm.
6. Ibid, emphasis added.
7. "Amanda Barnes Smith," mormonwiki.com/Amanda_Barnes_Smith.
8. Tullidge, ibid, emphasis added.
9. Ibid, emphasis added.
10. Ibid, emphasis added.
11. Smith, quoted in Emmeline B. Wells, "Amanda Smith," 189.
12. Smith, "O My Children and Grandchildren," 7.
13. Smith, History, 20, as quoted in Women of Faith in the Latter-days, 340.
14. "Amanda Barnes Smith," *Women of Faith*, 341.
15. Smith, quoted in Wells, "Amanda Smith," 13.

BIBLIOGRAPHY

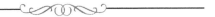

Anderson, Karl Ricks. *Joseph Smith's Kirtland, Eyewitnesses Accounts*. Salt Lake City: Deseret Book, 1989.

Andrus, Hyrum L. and Andrus, Helen Mae. *They Knew the Prophet*. Salt Lake City: Bookcraft, 1974.

Beecher, Maureen Ursenbach. *Eliza Roxy Snow, The Personal Writings of*. Logan, UT: Utah State University Press, 2000.

Black, Susan Easton and Woodger, Mary Jane. *Women of Character*. American Fork, UT: Covenant Communications, Inc., 2011.

Daughters in My Kingdom: The History and Work of Relief Society. Salt Lake City: The Church of Jesus Christ of Latter-day Saints, Intellectual Reserve, 2011.

Davidson, Karen Lynn and Derr, Jill Mulvay. *Eliza: The Life and Faith of Eliza R. Snow*. Salt Lake City: Deseret Book, 2013.

Davidson, Karen Lynn and Derr, Jill Mulvay. *Eliza R. Snow The Complete Poetry*. Provo, UT: Brigham Young University Press, 2009.

Gates, Susa Young. "Suffrage Won by the Mothers of the United States," *Relief Society Magazine*, May 1920.

Godfrey, Kenneth W., Godfrey, Audrey M., and Derr, Jull Mulvay. *Women's Voices: An Untold History of the Latter-day Saints 1830–1900*. Salt Lake City: Deseret Book, 1982.

Jakeman, Joseph T., ed. *Album Book: Daughters of Utah Pioneers and Their Mothers*. Salt Lake City: Daughters of Utah Pioneers, 1911.

Jones, Gracia N. *Emma's Glory and Sacrifice, a Testimony*. Homestead Publishers and Distributors, 1987.

Karras, Christy. *Remarkable Utah Women*. Morris Book Publishing, 2010.

Karras, Christy. *More than Petticoats: Remarkable Utah Women*. Lanham, MD: Globe Pequot, January 2010.

Kimball, Sarah M. "Auto-biography," *Woman's Exponent* 12, September 1, 1883.

Kimball, Sarah M. "Our Sixth Sense, or the Spiritual Understanding," *Woman's Exponent* 23, April 15, 1895.

Madsen, Carol Cornwall. *In Their Own Words*. Salt Lake City: Deseret Book, 1994.

McCloud, Susan Evans. *Joseph Smith, A Photobiography*. Aspen Books, 1992.

Rawson, Glenn. "The Indomitable Faith of Mary Fielding Smith," *LDS Living*, ldsliving.com/The-Indomitable-Faith-of-Mary-Fielding-Smith-How-Hyrum's-Martyrdom-Changed-Her-ever/s/90736, May 6, 2019.

Sessions, Patty Bartlett. Edited by Donna Toland Smart. *Mormon Midwife: The 1846–1888 Diaries of Patty Bartlett Sessions*. Logan, UT: Utah State University Press, 1997.

Smith, Barbara B. and Thatcher, Blythe Darlyn, eds. *Heroines of the Restoration*. Salt Lake City: Bookcraft, 1997.

Smart, Donnal Toland, ed. *Patty Bartlett Sessions*. Logan, UT: Utah State University Press, 1997.

Smith, Hulda. "O My Children and Grandchildren: An Account of the Sealing of Amanda Barnes Smith to Joseph Smith," *Nauvoo Journal*, vol. 4, 1992.

Smith, Joseph. *History of The Church of Jesus Christ of Latter-day Saints*. Edited by B. H. Roberts. 2d ed. rev., 7 vols. Salt Lake City: The Church of Jesus Christ of Latter-day Saints, 1932–51.

Smith, Lucy Mack. *The Revised and Enhanced History of Joseph Smith by His Mother*. Bookcraft, 1996.

Snow, Eliza R. "My Epitaph," *Times and Seasons*, vol. 4, no. 11, April 15, 1843.

Tullidge, Edward W. *The Women of Mormondom*, Project Gutenberg, eremita. di.uminho.pt/gutenberg/5/4/3/3/54335/54335-h/54335-h.htm.

Turley, Richard E. Jr. and Chapman, Brittan A., eds. *Women of Faith in the Latter Days, Volume One 1775–1820*. Salt Lake City: Deseret Book, 2011.

Wells, Quentin Thomas. *Defender: The Life of Daniel H. Wells*. Logan, UT: Utah State University Press, 2016.

Wells, EB. *Encyclopedia of Mormonism*. New York: Macmillan, 1559–1560, 1992—via BYU Library, Digital Collections.

Woods, Fred E. *Gathering to Nauvoo*. American Fork, UT: Covenant Communications, Inc., 2002.

ABOUT THE AUTHOR

SUSAN EVANS MCCLOUD IS A prolific and versatile writer, with more than fifty published books that range from historical fiction to mystery, nonfiction, and children's literature. She has written her own column for *Deseret News* and created many programs and songs for the Church's Young Women, seminary, genealogy, and other programs. She is poetic yet precise in her writing and research and offers outstanding examples of literature at its best. She is also the author of two of our most beloved hymns, "Lord, I Would Follow Thee" and "As Zion's Youth."

Susan has taught English and creative writing at a private school and has served as teacher and area board member for Daughters of the Utah Pioneers. She has six children, ten grandchildren, and eight great-grandchildren to date.

Works of
Susan Evans McCloud

Over the space of forty years, Susan Evans McCloud has published more than fifty books, covering an impressive variety of genres, from fiction and mystery to children's books, biography, and a volume of poetry entitled *Songs of Life*, as well as a bride's planner, a quote book on women, and one on the writings of Brigham Young.

She has written for both stage and screen and series on "Poets of the Restoration" and "History of the Hymns" for radio.lds.org. Susan has also written programs and songs for seminary and Young Women and has to her credit a variety of screenplays that include *John Baker's Last Race*.

For upward of fifteen years, Susan has written her own column for MormonTimes.com and has created lyrics for many Church programs—this gift culminating in two hymns in the hymnal that are so beloved of the Saints: "As Zion's Youth in Latter days" and "Lord, I Would Follow Thee."

Her versatility is impressive, all the more so because of the professional care of her works and the depth of love and spirit they reflect.